MW01285219

THE
HILLS
IN
OUR
LIVES

Establishing and Maintaining
a Clear Connection to God

JEFF D. COPELAND

HIGH BRIDGE BOOKS

...I remember where You found me,
I'm amazed by where I stand...

—Casting Crowns, "Love Moved First"

CONTENTS

ACKNOWLEDGMENTS

FOR GOD'S GLORY: IT WOULD BE REMISS OF ME IF I didn't first and foremost thank God for showering me with a love I never deserved, for never giving up His pursuit of me until I finally just couldn't run away anymore, and for protecting me from myself through all the years I spent thinking I was really a self-made man doing life on my own. I thank Him for arranging life's circumstances to leave me no other option than to finally take the path He created just for me which brought me to where I am in life with Him today. I'm grateful for those He brought into my life, and the doors He opened for me to be able to finish this project I never felt qualified to begin, much less complete. I can't understand why He loves me so much and I certainly never deserved the multitude of blessings He has showered upon my life. He is everything we will ever need and so much more, and my prayer is that by His strength I can shine His light in such a way as to illuminate that truth for others to see.

FOR MOM AND DAD: In hindsight, I can't even imagine parents doing a better or more thorough job of teaching God's truths to their children and/or demonstrating actually living your life for God than you guys did. I have no explanation or excuse for why I couldn't see and understand all you tried to show me back then. I took the longer road to get here, but finally by the grace of God alone, made it back the roots you planted in me so long ago. I'm sorry y'all didn't live long enough to see this version of me on Earth, but I know you have a big hug waiting for me when we next meet, just like you always did while you were here. I can't wait for that day! Thanks for everything I took for granted growing up.

FOR MY PRAYING CHRISTIAN FRIENDS: For fear of leaving someone off the list, I'm not naming names, but you guys know who you are. Thank all of you for the living examples you provided me, the words of truth and encouragement you shared with me through the time we've been acquainted and the prayers I'm sure you were beginning to think were wasted breath over the years. And directly to the one who just finally just came right out and said, "I have never seen God chasing anyone as hard as I see Him chasing you" … I have no words except thank you for your boldness in that moment. I owe you guys a debt I can never repay, other than perhaps by trying to pay it forward. God surely has a special reward awaiting you on the other side of the pearly gates for never giving up on me.

INTRODUCTION

I'M ASKING YOU TO JOIN ME ON A JOURNEY IN SEARCH of our absolute best life. You know how when you go on a great vacation—one that turns out to be everything you had hoped for and more— you just can't imagine having a better time; and when it's time to go home, you feel kinda sad that the vacation is over? Tomorrow you must go back to work. And maybe it will be a whole year before you get to have that much fun and joy again.

The journey I'm inviting you on isn't like that. It is as much fun and full of joy as the vacation … but it never ends. And here is the kicker … you don't have to go anywhere to have all that fun and fullness of joy. You get to have it bursting out from inside you, spilling over onto others … all day, every day, FOREVER!

No, I'm not trying to sell you oceanfront property in Arizona. This is real and readily available! It is perfectly legal and is available to you no matter your current life circumstances. And it doesn't cost one red cent. In fact, it cannot be purchased with money. It's not for sale, but I promise you anyone can have it.

Do I have your interest and attention yet? Good! I am sure I also have a large pile of your suspicion as well, but that's ok and understandable. Not so long ago, if someone had made this proposition to me, I would have likely turned and ran, screaming for the hills, knowing that this sounds too good to be true and no such deal exists … Yet here I stand today, walking in the very life I'm describing.

In no way do I claim that I got here on my own, or in my own strength. It is not possible for me to do so; and it is not possible for you either. But I have found the source of power that not only is capable of getting us there, but assures us of reaching this place of peace and joy with a 100 percent iron-clad guarantee, backed by the strength of the Creator of the universe. If we learn to follow this plan, we never have to face fear, anxiety, depression, or any other negative human emotion again. We can live out our lives in a fullness of joy and peace that we can't even comprehend. If this life sounds too good to be true, you don't know my God. Please settle in and allow me to introduce you to Him and tell you how to find this destination.

In this book, I will share biblically grounded truth along with real-life experiences that will:

- Create a life-changing sense of awe for the power and love of God

- Help you understand and see the truth of biblical promises in your everyday life

- Teach you how to seek and find a real relationship with God

- Explain exactly how Biblical promises work

- Show you how to get/keep your focus on God and eliminate the issues of pride and self from your life

- Allow you to see how you can live a stress-free life

Our biggest hindrance to living the life the Bible promises is learning to get out of our own way. The promises from the Bible are ALL true! EVERYTIME! *The Hills in Our Lives* is an easy-to-understand roadmap for forming a real relationship with God and living your best life … the life of peace and joy!

> I do not cease to give thanks for you, remembering you in my prayers, that the God of our Lord Jesus Christ, the Father of glory, may give you the Spirit of wisdom and of revelation in the knowledge of him, having the eyes of your hearts enlightened, that you may know what is the hope to which he has called you, what are the riches of his glorious inheritance in the saints, and what is the immeasurable greatness of his power toward us who believe, according to the working of his great might that he worked in Christ when he raised him from the dead and seated him at his right hand in the heavenly places, far above all rule and authority and power and dominion, and above every name that is named, not only in this age but also in the one to come. And he put all things under his feet and gave him as head over all things to the church, which

is his body, the fullness of him who fills all in all. (Ephesians 1:16-23)

Amen.

1

HILLS IN MY LIFE...

THE HILLS IN OUR LIVES STORY IS THE CULMINATION of an unbelievably amazing chapter of struggle in my life! I was in a huge battle with depression for about four years after my wife of twenty years left me without warning in January of 2014. That was the straw that broke the camel's back and caused me to hit rock bottom, which is where I found God waiting for me ... more about that later.

After several months of just being in shock over what happened, I had isolated myself by moving onto a 20,000-acre hunting ranch in the Texas Hill Country, where I worked as a hunting guide. Since I could do most of what was required at the ranch in my sleep, this move afforded me lots of time to work on ... or rather learn to let God work on ... rebuilding me into the person He had designed me to be all along. As my walk with Him and my faith began to grow, I started seeing life differently ... through the lens of His eyes! However, no matter how good I was doing, any time a string of 7-20 straight days of hunting would end, I'd find myself exhausted and would end up feeling lonely and depressed because I didn't understand why my life was falling apart. I talked to God about what happened a lot, but the cycle just kept on repeating itself, over and over, like I was living in the movie *Groundhog Day.*

Finally, January 6, 2019, I'd finished up a hunt the day before and went to church in Utopia, Texas. Service was great, and I came out all happy and feeling "full of Jesus." I hadn't been home in a couple weeks, so I decided I'd go straight from there to Bandera to check my PO box and check on my house. I had my radio tuned to Christian radio station KLove, as always, and I was driving through the hills, just happily singing praises and continuing my morning worship.

I don't know if you've ever driven from Utopia to Bandera on FM 470, but it's a very winding, little two-lane road that cuts through some really rugged hills along the way. Every time the terrain would dip, I'd start having static or other stations bleeding in over my KLove. Needless to say, it didn't take much of that distraction to "harsh my mellow" and finally, just begin to irritate me.

I yelled irreverently, "GOD! I'm just trying to sing praises to You! Why can't I just hear my station and sing to You?!!!"

A soft, little voice replied from somewhere deep in my soul. "It's the hills interfering with the radio wave transmissions."

"I know!" I replied, "But You're God! Aren't You powerful enough to help the signal get to me when You know I need it?!!!"

The soft, little voice answered, "It's the same problem you keep having with your shifting moods and feelings of loneliness. You have hills in your life. They cause you to take your focus off of Me. You forget that I am always with you ... just like when your radio loses its signal as you drive through the hills. This is the lesson you need to seek answers for so you can share the truth with others in the same struggle. Don't let the hills in your life break your communion with Me!"

To say the least, I was beyond humbled and stunned at the revelation, and I didn't ask any more questions on the rest of the drive home. And oddly, my radio never lost signal again the remainder of that trip.

I had pondered that conversation a lot in the year since it happened. Almost a year to the day, I was again tired and driving through the hills and sure enough, right in the middle of one of my favorite songs, a Spanish station started bleeding in and out, completely ruining my holy peace. Forgetting my humility momentarily, I banged on my dash and cried out, "God! Not now! I love this song, and I need it right now!"

That same, quiet, little voice replied again, "When you're trying to commune with Me and the hills interrupt, it's really irritating, isn't it?"

A bit bewildered at the thought, I answered, "YES!!! Exactly!"

Then the little voice said, "I'm trying to commune with you 24/7, but you're still allowing the hills in your life to interrupt all that I'm trying to do in, for, and through you."

That drove the point home to me! God created man to need God and have constant communion in our walk with Him through this short amount of time we get to spend here on Planet Earth, before we are joined with Him forever in the land of no more sorrows, tears, or death (Revelation 21:4). He is INFINITELY good and wants nothing more than to lead us down the perfect path He has created just for each of us as individuals. This is so we can learn for ourselves and show others how to fully engage with Him, enjoying the life of immeasurable grace, peace, and joy that He has designed for us all. I have come to realize that we mess that all up on a daily, if not hourly, basis.

For the last several years, I have been on a quest to remedy that problem in my own life. I have made progress and learned a lot. The main thing I have learned is that I am not very good at holding up my end of the deal, but none of us are, as Romans 3:23 so clearly points out:

> For all have sinned and fall short of the glory of God!

Luckily for us, God is infinitely perfect at holding up His end of the deal, so much so that He has provided us with a foolproof means of staying forever under His grace, despite our continual failure to live up to His standard. That is the message I pray I can articulate clearly and simply enough for you to take away from this book.

I'll state right here in the introduction that as a person in my own strength and knowledge, I, by no means, feel even remotely qualified to write such a manuscript for life. If I were God, there are lots of people who are far more versed in the Scriptures who I might have chosen to attempt to deliver this message. But for some reason, the need I feel to pen these words just refuses to diminish, even though I have fought the urge for a couple years now. That said, I am just trying to let the thoughts flow from my soul to my computer without trying to filter them through my own brain. Since I don't feel that God called the qualified for this project, I am trusting that He will qualify the one He called and praying that He uses these words to illuminate the message to you in such a way as to bring you to His place of peace that truly surpasses human understanding (Philippians 4:6-9). As I am learning daily, it really is an awesome place to live your best life, and more and more, I find that my circumstances (good or bad, easy or difficult) have no bearing on the peace in my soul, or the joy in my heart, just as the apostle Paul stated in Philippians 4:11-13:

> Not that I am speaking of being in need, for I have learned in whatever situation I am to be content. I know how to be brought low, and I know how to abound. In any and every

circumstance, I have learned the secret of facing plenty and hunger, abundance and need. I can do all things through him who strengthens me.

My prayer is that when you read this book, you'll be equipped with every tool you need to join me in this awesome place of peace.

Father, we thank You for Your infinite grace and mercy, and for the good plan You've created for our lives. As we begin this journey, seeking to identify and eliminate the hills from our lives, which cause us to, even momentarily, shift our focus off of You and onto our circumstances, we ask that You open our eyes and hearts to allow us to see and taste that You are good so that we can become the blessed one who takes refuge in You alone (Psalm 34:8). Grant us wisdom and faith to understand and believe that You truly work all things for the good of those who love You and are called according to Your purpose (Romans 8:28). Humble us in Your presence, Lord, and give us the strength to get out of our own way, and out of Your way, so that You can make us more like Christ and use us to the fullest extent in our mission to glorify Your name ... and let us begin to comprehend the immense peace and joy that comes from yielding to You in all that we do. In Jesus's mighty name, we pray. Amen.

2

How This Journey Began for Me

ONE THING I HAVE LEARNED FOR AN ABSOLUTE CERtainty: there are no accidents or coincidences in this life! I have come to realize that everything that happens to us has a purpose. Everyone who crosses our path is led through by God's plan, either to help or teach us ... or to be helped or taught by us ... or some combination thereof. We can't always see it at the time, but it is ALWAYS true!

I walked through most of my life focused on self, with self always at the center. I thought I was the only one who I could truly depend on one hundred percent. I was strong and determined, and successful at everything I did. I lived life on my own terms, asked nobody for help, and looked down on "weaker" people who always seemed to "need" help, even with things in life they should be able to fix themselves. When adversity came, I'd curse the God I didn't really even believe in, lick my wounds, burn those bridges, and keep plodding forward. "Suck it up and move on" was my mantra!

Problem was, even though I had burned the bridges, I never forgave anyone ... ever! So, as I moved on, I'd pack all that dirty, emotional baggage up with all the rest I had accumulated throughout my life, heft it up on my strong, self-reliant shoulders, and move out. Long story short, at 47-48 years old, that load just got too heavy for even me to carry, and it crushed me like a bug. I couldn't do it anymore and found myself as low in the depths of depression as a human can go. That was the first time in my life where being the consummate over-thinker actually served me well.

Literally, sitting at rock bottom, note written and seconds short of pulling the trigger, I saw God's outstretched hand and finally realized He had been there through every detail of my life, providing all the strengths for every victory I'd ever had in life that I had claimed as my own. I suddenly saw with 20/20 hindsight, all the little (and big) adversities He had let me stumble across, as efforts to squelch my pride and attempts to cause me to realize my insufficiency and my need for Him ... I suddenly saw ALL I needed to have done differently ... different decisions, different attitudes ... that would have allowed me to grow and flourish as a person, instead of being slowly overloaded with all the negative baggage I insisted on shouldering while continuing forward in life. My fall was destined to happen; it was the only potential outcome possible, given the decisions I was making.

I didn't know it, but I needed humbling. I needed God to jerk the rug out from under me and knock me to my knees. I was hard-headed, but thankfully, He had finally succeeded in showing me that apart from Him, I could literally do nothing (John 15:5). When I saw God's outstretched hand and was granted the clarity to see and acknowledge all of this, I begged His forgiveness for my pride and obstinance. I told Him I was done trying to do life on my own, my way, in my own strength. I thanked Him for not ever giving up on me, even though I definitely deserved His wrath and abandonment. Then, I asked Him to flood and fill all the holes in my heart, while taking control of my life and leading me in whatever direction He wanted me to go.

God had spent sooo many years blessing me without acknowledgement from me, giving me everything a man could have wanted in this life ... and I'd squandered it all, chasing "my neon rainbow" and thinking I was doing it all on my own.

From the beginning, He had lain out the perfect plan for my life. All I ever needed to do was take His hand and walk alongside Him, being blessed the whole way ... but no! I had to take every trial and every hardship as a personal attack on me ... as if the universe was out to get me. Just me against the world. I was an idiot! I can see so clearly now, every intersection where adversity came along was nothing more than an opportunity for growth that I shunned and dismissed. God had been trying to nudge me along, back toward His intended plan and path my whole life, but I just continued to snub my nose at Him and forge along "my own" path. If any of this sounds familiar to your own life, don't get discouraged, but take heart. There is a way out of your troubles.

The further away from His path I got, the stronger the nudges became ... heftier adversities, weightier decisions, with more dire consequences, seemingly at every intersection. And I ignored ALL the signs ... until a Christian friend finally just came out and told me point blank, "I've never seen God chasing someone as hard as I see Him chasing you!"

I was floored ... and her words echoed through my psyche, haunting me twenty-four hours a day for months. God bless her for uttering these words, because that statement was the one insight that finally caught my attention and made me stop and think. Her words, and the weight and authority with which she said them, forced me to consider the possibility that perhaps I was indeed running in the wrong direction. Her statement and my OCD, overthinking nature are the things that finally drove me to the beginnings of my asking, seeking, and knocking (Matthew 7:7-8).

THIS level of humility before God is the starting point to the greatest peace you will ever know in this life, and the most critical decision you can ever make in your life! If you've accepted Christ as your Savior and begun your walk with Him toward eternity, you know what I'm saying. If you have not made this decision, or if you are unsure if you have made this decision, I'm gonna ask you to do so now. It's not hard. John 3:16-17 states:

> For God so loved the world, that he gave his only Son, that whoever believes in him should not perish but have eternal life. For God did not send his Son into the world to condemn the world, but in order that the world might be saved through him.

Romans 10:9-10 states:

> If you confess with your mouth that Jesus is Lord and believe in your heart that God raised him from the dead, you will be saved. For with the heart one believes and is justified, and with the mouth one confesses and is saved.

Romans 10:13 states:

> For everyone who calls on the name of the Lord will be saved.

It's really just that simple. All you have to do is believe in your heart that God sent His Son Jesus to die for our sins and raised Him from the dead. Ask Him to come into your heart, and He will. For anything else to make sense in the rest of this book, you have to first make this decision. Without having Jesus in your life, and growing in your relationship with Him, you will never make it to the place I'm trying to describe for you. Even if you've already accepted Christ as your Savior, pray this prayer with me now:

> *Father God, we ask that You open our eyes right now, and allow us to see ourselves exactly where we are in our relationship with You at this moment. If we have not yet accepted Your offer of eternal life with You through the precious blood of Jesus Christ, reveal to us the truth that He is the way, the truth, and the life, and that there is no other way into Your presence and peace (John 14:6). In Jesus's name we ask, Amen.*

If you are ready to receive Christ, pray this prayer with me right now:

> *Dear Heavenly Father, forgive me of my sins and wash me clean in the blood of Jesus. I'm tired of fighting life on my own, and I want to live the good plan You have for my life. I believe that Jesus came and died in my place to pay for my sins, and that you raised Him from the dead. I give my life to You and ask You to help me grow to be more like Christ, and use me to glorify Your name. In Jesus's name, Amen.*

If you prayed that prayer just now with a sincere heart, God answered it as it came from your lips. Your sins are forgiven and remembered no more (Hebrews 8:12; 1 John 1:9). You are a child of God (Romans 8:16), and He will never leave you or forsake you (Hebrews 13:5). Embrace those facts. Look up the verses and read them for yourself, and remind yourself of them every morning. It will help grow your faith ... and FAITH is the key to helping eliminate the hills from your life. We'll get to that concept shortly. Congratulations on making the best decision of your life!!!

3

SO, WHAT ARE THE HILLS IN OUR LIVES?

FTER MY FIRST ENCOUNTER WITH THE SOFT, LITTLE voice described in my introduction, I began thinking a lot about what made up the hills in my own life. I've already named one, and it was a BIG one for me ... unforgiveness.

When I finally learned the lesson, it came as a shock to me that forgiveness was really such an important character trait. My whole life, I had operated under the mistaken mantra of "Time heals all wounds." This is a total untruth! Time doesn't actually heal anything but puts space and distance between you and whatever/whomever "injured or wronged" you.

Over time, your anger or hurt may indeed seem to subside because you no longer constantly dwell on the event, but sometimes, years or even decades later, if something happens to remind you of the event, you will find yourself instantly feeling just as angry/hurt as you were the day it happened. That is not healing. The truth of the matter is unless you learn to forgive, truly forgive, and let go of such things, they just become emotional baggage that you carry around for the rest of your life until it gets so heavy that it crushes you.

Unforgiveness creates an infection of bitterness in your soul over time. If left unchecked and not properly dealt with, this infection will eventually cause problems in your future relationships (if it doesn't destroy them altogether like it did mine). It will also definitely break your communion with God, which leaves you right back at the point where I found myself ... plodding my own frustratingly rocky course through life, under my own strength, all alone and very far from the path of blessing that God had intended for me to walk with Him.

Forgiveness is the antibiotic that cures the infection of bitterness! That revelation should not have been such a shock to me, since the Bible speaks so much on the subject (Matthew 6:14-15; Colossians 3:13; Ephesians 4:31-32). Had I spent my whole life studying the Word like I do now, I certainly would have grasped this concept before it destroyed my life. But like I stated earlier, I was doing life my way, on my terms, and didn't realize how much I needed to just sit down and read the instruction manual from God.

Now, some of you reading this may be walking a path similar to the one I was on, and if so, I can hear you thinking to yourself right now, *Well, you don't know how bad they hurt me and you don't know how unforgivable what they did to me was.* Am I right? Bear with me for a moment, because I'm going to tell you that no matter what they did to you … it just doesn't matter. You see, forgiveness isn't even about the other person. It's about you. You never even have to tell the other person that you forgive them. BUT you do have to forgive them to cure the spiritual infection of bitterness … which is exactly what caused you to make the statement above. Don't stress about it though; I'm going to tell you exactly how to go about forgiving the unforgivable, even those most painful things for which you never received an apology!

If you are just beginning your walk with Christ, it may take a little time and spiritual growth before this statement really sinks in, but the key to being able to forgive the unforgivable is to understand and become in awe of how God forgives us. It takes some Bible study, but once your mind wraps around exactly how much we sin … daily, and exactly how truly short we fall from the glory of God (Romans 3:23) … daily, and then wraps around how much exactly God loves us and forgives us anyway, and the lengths He went to, just to provide for our salvation; being in awe of His love for us and the way He forgives us just spontaneously surfaces in your conscience. I encourage you to spend time daily reading the Bible to see many examples for yourself, but just to give you a glimpse into what I'm saying here, let's look briefly at Romans 5:6-8:

> For while we were still weak, at the right time, Christ died for the ungodly. For one will scarcely die for a righteous person – though perhaps for a good person one would dare even to die – but God shows his love for us in that while we were still sinners, Christ died for us.

Think about that and let it soak in for a minute. From Adam and Eve forward, all of us are born sinners. We lie and cheat and steal and curse and blaspheme the name of the God who created us and the world we live in. God gives us life and breath, feeding us and clothing us. He designed the best life path for us ... just for us ... before time began, and how do we repay Him? We refuse to do His will and forge our own paths through life that can only lead us straight into hell, with no chance that we will ever join Him in heaven, even if we are trying to be good. We should be utterly detestable to Him ... but instead, He loves us so much that in His desire to forgive us and give us a chance to join Him in heaven, He sent His Son to die a horrible, shameful death on a cross to pay the penalty for ALL of OUR sins. He then raised Him from the dead and tells us the only thing we have to do to get His total forgiveness, and receive ALL His blessings, is to confess our sins and believe that He sent His Son to be destroyed for our sake. Friends, that is LOVE and FORGIVENESS beyond measure!

When that concept sinks in and is understood, if it doesn't create a sense of awe in you, nothing will. We deserve to die and be separated from God forever! We defy and disappoint Him every single day of our lives ... but we can't seem to make Him stop loving and forgiving us. When you understand that concept, you can't wait to forgive others ... even if they don't deserve it!

I urge you to spend time every day reading your Bible until you grasp the kind of unending love that God has for us. It is truly mind-boggling, and this love can't help but change your life for the better. Holding onto grudges, unforgiveness, and bitterness creates weights on you that you honestly can't believe how heavy they are until you learn how to really forgive and let go. The weight of bitterness increases so gradually over time, you don't really notice it but it is always there, making you tired, grouchy, and depressed, little by little, until one day you just can't get up anymore. You won't even know why you feel the way you do ... at least I didn't. When I finally came to the realization and learned how to forgive ... everything, I swear it literally felt like an elephant stepped off my chest, and I could breathe for the first time in years.

Ok, I spent a lot of time there discussing forgiveness. I'm not quite done yet, but let's address some of other possible hills in our lives. The list I came up with for myself included stress, pressure, anxiety, worry, depression, responsibility, jobs, bills, debts, expectations, selfishness, fear, pride, idols, and sin. I'm sure this list is incomplete, even for me. Your own list may contain even more items or less. There is no cookie-cutter list because as individuals, we are all created differently, live different lives, and have different experiences. I went in depth discussing unforgiveness because in my own life, that was a huge issue I had to deal with before I could even clearly see the other issues. I'll tell you one other thing about forgiveness before I move on and give you the secret to dealing with all of the above-mentioned, and any other obstacles you may encounter along the path you choose through life.

It struck me as odd that the most difficult person to grant forgiveness to was myself. The day I learned the importance of forgiveness, I literally sat down with a notepad and made a list of everyone I could remember from my whole forty-eight-year life who had ever done something I had failed to forgive them for. I listed them chronologically to the best of my ability, from most recent to oldest ... (yes, I'm a little bit OCD). It was pages, lots of people, representing lots of grudges and bitterness, some having carried on for decades. I was being totally honest with myself, and the strangest thing I found about my list was that the first name included was my own. I had to forgive myself for my part in the failure of my marriage. Then, to top it all off, my name was also the last one on the list, because I felt the need to forgive myself for my failure to handle all these other issues in a timely and appropriate manner throughout my life. That was because the weight of carrying all that bitterness around for so long was ultimately the cause of me morphing into a depressed, miserable, and self-centered person who my wife felt the necessity to abandon.

So, I went through my list, emptying all the bitterness, hurt, and anger from my heart. As I mentioned, it felt like an elephant stepped off my chest. The relief was immense and immediate, as I put all that behind me and let God have it to deal with as He saw fit. I was elated with myself for finally coming to this understanding ... BUT ... a few days later, I found myself feeling down and kinda beating myself up about being so stupid and carrying that stuff around for so long, letting it cause problems in my marriage. This was a first for me. I had never experienced this feeling of insufficiency before. I was realizing I needed God as my source of strength in my life. So I prayed about it. I asked God to forgive me again, felt better about it for a few days ... AND ... then it would happen again. I'd go through the same process. I did it so many times that I felt like the instructions on a shampoo bottle: lather, rinse, repeat. Then it dawned on me: you gotta stop and get out of the shower!

What was I missing here? Why couldn't I get out of the cycle? Why could I not let my own transgressions go, like I had those of all the others who made up my list? The answer I found is the KEY ... not just the key to forgiveness, but the key to conquering and flattening ALL the hills in our lives: the KEY to unlocking real peace and joy in life. I'm talking about THE peace and joy that the Bible promises is available to all of us who belong to Christ, yet so many of us seem unable to find! YES!!! This is where you want to start taking notes, because what I am about to reveal is the truth about why people struggle through life sad, tired, and depressed, lacking optimism, happiness, hope, peace, and the fullness of joy that we as Christians are promised and entitled to. Despite the fallen world we inhabit, and the harsh circumstances we sometimes find ourselves in the midst of, this hope, peace, and fullness of joy truly does exist. It's readily and handily available, regardless of even our worst possible circumstances, just like the Bible promises. We just don't understand how to find and grab hold of the truth in the Bible.

I realize that is a mighty bold blanket statement I just made about the secret to flattening EVERY hill, in every life, with a single key, but I promise it is the absolute truth ... and it is a hundred percent trustworthy and foolproof! I know that statement sounds too good to be true, and it actually is too good to be true ... BUT ... that is the God we serve. He is too good to be true, but true He is. He is awe-inspiring. Now, these revelations didn't jump out of my Bible all at once. Instead, it evolved through a diligent amount of asking, seeking, and knocking (Matthew 7:7-11) on my part. To demonstrate how I got there, allow me to finish my story of self-forgiveness from above. Then, I will show you how it works, across the board for any issue life might throw at you.

Around the, I don't know, three hundredth time I was passing through the cycle of beating myself up and asking God to forgive me once again, I finally prayed, "God! Why does this same circumstance keep cycling back and plaguing me? Why can't I let it go?" Suddenly, three scriptures just popped into my head out of nowhere, bam, bam, bam ... in this order:

> If we confess our sins, he is faithful and just to forgive us our sins and to cleanse us from all unrighteousness. (1 John 1:9)
>
> For I will be merciful toward their iniquities, and I will remember their sins no more. (Hebrews 8:12)

...But one thing I do: forgetting what lies behind and straining forward to what lies ahead, I press on toward the goal for the prize of the upward call of God in Christ Jesus.
(Philippians 3:13-14)

Stunned ... I stopped mid-prayer. I had already confessed this sin 299-ish other times ... which meant God had forgiven this sin as the first confession parted my lips (1 John 1:9). At that very moment of His forgiveness upon my utterance of the first confession, He had also put this bothersome sin of mine in the past and out of His mind (Hebrews 8:12). He was done with it ... which meant that I also was supposed to be done with it. Instead of continuing to cycle through feeling guilty about it, repenting again and again ... I was supposed to be forgetting what lies behind and straining forward to what lies ahead (Philippians 3:13-14). And then it hit me... This is how the promises in the Bible work!

If God has forgiven me and put my sin in the past to remember it no more ... who am I to keep on remembering it, beating myself up about it, and bugging Him to "forgive me again and again" for it? After my first confession, He doesn't even know what I'm whining about to Him the other 299 times, because He "remembers it no more!" I realized I had spent the preceding three months (or maybe it was six months?) wasting so much energy and time, beating myself up and feeling guilty and unforgiven for something God had already dealt with and put behind US ... me AND Him. I was, in effect, sinning by not receiving His forgiveness, and in doing so, I was making myself miserable by not walking in the forgiveness He had granted. I was once again forging my own path through the rockiest of grounds, while He had plowed a smooth road for me to walk WITH Him, six inches away from where I was struggling!

Father, we don't have words to express the gratitude due for the love You have shown us. We are totally undeserving of the mercy and grace You have freely offered us through the blood of Jesus. You know we are a fallen people living in a fallen world. You know in the weakness of our own understanding, we will never be able to grasp and attain the life You desire for us to live under Your covenant of grace. We thank You for sending our helper, the Holy Spirit, to live in our hearts to help guide us into becoming the person You designed us to be, living the life You planned for us to live. Please grant us wisdom and show us through Your eyes how to walk in this life, as we seek to become more like Christ. In the name of Jesus we ask, Amen.

4

IT HELPS TO KNOW

I SPENT A LOT OF TIME IN THAT LAST CHAPTER SHOWING you exactly how I battled through flattening my hill of unforgiveness; that IS exactly how ALL the promises in the Bible work. We learn them... We trust them... And then we walk in them. When we do, we will find they work a hundred percent of the time. Just before Jesus died on the cross, He stated, "IT IS FINISHED!" (John 19:30). What He meant by that victorious exclamation is that His mission on earth was complete. He had paid the price for all the sins of the world, and His blood had signed, sealed, delivered, and guaranteed the new covenant being given to all believers. All debts cancelled, all promises delivered. This is important for you to understand in order for you to grasp what I am about to tell you next.

There are no external hills in our lives!

You read that correctly. There are no external hills in our lives. The list I came up with for myself including unforgiveness, stress, pressure, anxiety, worry, depression, responsibility, jobs, bills, debts, expectations, selfishness, fear, pride, idols, and sin, plus whatever other items you may have come up with in your own self-examination. These are not external hills. Those things are all circumstances and roadblocks that we create for ourselves. *We are* the hills in our own lives!

God is *always* here with us, and His promises are *always* available for us to claim and use. He has given us His Word as an instruction manual for life. In the Bible, He has told us all the promises, showing us through the story of the cross and the resurrection how Jesus has completed all the work to fulfill all of those promises and paid the entire debt of our sin. We either don't understand it, we forget it, or we just don't believe it.

I mentioned earlier that my revelation of the single key for flattening all the hills in my life didn't just pop out of my Bible right away. Instead, it is an understanding of how God's promises will work in our lives without fail that has evolved for me one tiny step at a time, over the course of several years. I'll illustrate more as we follow the threads, but I want to make sure you understand how I finally came into full forgiveness. I outlined it in detail above. I had been reading and studying my Bible every day for a couple years at that point, *but I had still somehow missed the point I was supposed to have gleaned from God's Word on how forgiveness works and how to take rest in it.*

Rather than taking rest in the promises of God on the subject, I was still giving my power over to the enemy, allowing him to wreak havoc in my mind with feelings of guilt and shame over the things in the past. The devil would whisper into my subconscious, "Remember what a horrible person you were? Remember how self-centered you were and how you wrecked your life?" And suddenly, I would find myself joining in and telling myself how badly I had messed up my life, and how ignorant I was … instead of just punching him in the face with 1 John 1:9 and telling him to get away from me before I hit him again with Hebrews 8:12 and Philippians 3:13-14. That is exactly what I should have done because that is how we are supposed to fight our battles. The secret for that to happen is I must first have recognized I was under attack. We must learn to be ever vigilant in that regard. Jesus Himself told us:

> The thief comes only to steal, kill and destroy. I came that they
> may have life and have it abundantly. (John 10:10)

Once we have given our lives to Christ, the enemy has no more authority over us on this earth. Take a look at some scriptures on the subject:

> Submit yourselves therefore to God. Resist the devil, and he
> will flee from you. (James 4:7-8)

> Behold, I have given you authority to tread on serpents and
> scorpions, and over all the power of the enemy, and nothing
> shall hurt you. (Luke 10:19)

Little children, you are from God and have overcome them, for he who is in you is greater than he who is in the world. (1 John 4:4)

For though we walk in the flesh, we are not waging war according to the flesh. For the weapons of our warfare are not of the flesh but have divine power to destroy strongholds. [We will visit the subject of strongholds later.] We destroy arguments and every lofty opinion raised against the knowledge of God, and take every thought captive to obey Christ. (2 Corinthians 10:3-5)

For everyone who has been born of God overcomes the world. And this is the victory that has overcome the world – our faith. Who is it that overcomes the world except the one who believes that Jesus is the Son of God. (1 John 5:4-5)

There are many other examples. We just don't understand, believe, and use the power and authority we have through our relationship with Jesus Christ. Also important to remember: just because the enemy has no authority over us doesn't mean that he will not constantly be looking for the opportunity to trick us into giving him back our power. Just like the promises in the Bible about forgiveness (which I had read so many times but failed to digest and take personally to heart), there are also promises in the Bible about every other circumstance we will ever face in life. But we must learn those promises and trust them, or they just won't work for us in our lives. There are illicit warnings about various tactics the enemy will use to attack us and details on how we can successfully thwart every attempt he makes to steal our peace. We just, for some reason, as broken humans in a fallen world can't seem to follow the directions given to us in the Bible.

I've come to the conclusion that the reasons for this behavior can be boiled down into this oversimplified statement: *Lots of people believe IN God ... but very few people actually BELIEVE God.* It is a true statement as much for Christians as it is for non-believers!

Now don't take that statement the wrong way. I am by no means judging others, or claiming I am any better at *believing* God myself than the next guy. I struggle with this every single day of my life, and I know better. I have learned and used many of the promises I have found in the Bible ... and seen them work exactly as stated, a hundred percent of the times I have pulled them out and wielded them as weapons ... yet I still find myself on occasion feeling depressed, or anxious, or guilty. I still fall victim to even the feeblest and lamest attacks from the enemy. I sin and fall short of the glory of God every single day (Romans 8:23). It irks and disappoints me to admit it, but it is true. Every time it happens, I repent and ask God to help me remember to be stronger in His promises the next time. Having a real relationship with God that includes true communion and produces the real peace that is promised us in the Scriptures requires diligent effort on our part ... BUT it IS SO WORTH the effort! The result is that even in our failures, we are still blessed by God!

If you find yourself wearing those same frustratingly uncomfortable shoes, don't be too hard on yourself. Believe me when I tell you that I am writing this book as much to, and for, myself as I am writing it to share these truths with the world for God's glory. Also believe me when I tell you that as struggling, fallen humans, we are in good company. And yes, the Bible addresses this obstacle as well. The apostle Paul discussed constantly finding himself in the same battle. Check out what he says in Romans 7:14-25:

> For we know that the law is spiritual, but I am of the flesh, sold under sin. For I do not understand my own actions. For I do not do what I want, but I do the very thing I hate. Now if I do what I do not want, I agree with the law, that it is good. So now it is no longer I who do it, but sin that dwells within me. For I know that nothing good dwells in me, that is, in my flesh. For I have the desire to do what is right, but not the ability to carry it out. For I do not do the good I want, but the evil I do not want is what I keep on doing. Now if I do what I do not want, it is no longer I who do it, but sin that dwells within me. So I find it to be a law that when I want to do right, evil lies close at hand. For I delight in the law of God, in my inner being, but I see in my members another law waging war against the law of my mind and making me captive to the law of sin that dwells in my members. Wretched man that I am! Who will deliver me from this body of death? Thanks be to God through Jesus Christ our Lord! So then, I myself serve the law of God with my mind, but with my flesh I serve the law of sin.

Again, that was the apostle Paul ... and he penned over half of the New Testament. The Word of God was revealed to him by God personally on the road to Damascus and revealed in such a profound manner that Paul's whole identity (even his name) was immediately transformed on the spot! If after such a dramatic revelation and transformation, even Paul had to continue to diligently work to maintain his communion with God, how much more will we?

Kind and righteous Heavenly Father, we kneel before You in humility as fallen humans seeking Your will for our lives. We thank You that You so willingly for-give our stumbling each time we approach Your throne of grace. We ask that You fuel our hunger for Your Word and through Your Holy Spirit, which resides in us. We ask that You illuminate Your promises so that they resonate in our souls as we read them, so that we can keep them close at hand and learn to lean on them for strength to offset our weaknesses, as we strive to stay on the path You have made smooth for us. In Jesus's mighty name we pray, AMEN.

5

WHY IS IT SO HARD FOR US TO WALK IN THE PROMISES OF GOD?

IN CHAPTER 1, I SHARED WITH YOU MY REVELATION about the hills in my life. Pastor Robert Richarz from Living Waters Church in Utopia, Texas (www.thewaterhole.net), recently shared a similar analogy in a message. He likened our spiritual journey through life to driving through the Hill Country on a foggy pre-dawn morning. As the road twists and turns, rises and dips through the hills and valleys, we struggle to see and stay on the road with our headlights in the fog. We are on full alert as the fog reflects our headlights back into our faces, while watching for curves along with the threat of deer/hogs darting out in front of our vehicles. It's hard to see ahead through the fog. Then, as the terrain ascends or descends above or below the level of the fog, suddenly everything is clear, and driving is easy and comfortable. But once our elevation again changes, the fog blinds us again. If you've ever had the experience of driving through the Texas Hill Country, you know how such conditions can persist for miles and miles.

This is the perfect analogy for how our faith ebbs and flows in our feeble human attempts to walk through our lives with Christ. And there are a number of reasons we fall into pits in life, or find ourselves trying to climb a hill that seems too steep on the path we have chosen, or find ourselves passing in and out of the fog through a particular section of life. More so in modern times than in any other human era, our fast-paced, stress-filled, technologically-advanced lifestyles seem to be reinforcing the false connotation that we just don't have time for God, especially close communion with God. The more we follow this logic, dictated by our modern lifestyle, the more strained our relationship with God becomes ... and this is totally to our detriment. God is still the same omnipotent, self-sufficient, sovereign Being that He has ALWAYS been ... and we are still very much, more so than ever, none of those things.

God is not some genie in a bottle who, in times of our need, can just be summoned to grant us a wish and then be placed back on a shelf until our next crisis. Instead, He created us to need and want a real relationship with Him. He created us to need, want, and seek to have communion with Him. The definition of communion is "the sharing or exchange of intimate thoughts and feelings, especially when the exchange is on a mental or spiritual level."[1] The simple fact of the matter is that having communion with God is the only thing that will ever truly satisfy the human soul (Psalm 16:11, Psalm 107:9, John 6:35, John 7:38). That is the reason why so many extremely wealthy people, who seem to have everything, end up lonely, bitter, and depressed. And it is important to note in that definition of communion that it is a "sharing or exchange" of intimate thoughts and feelings, which means that our communion with God is not just us talking to Him in prayer. It also includes our listening to, hearing, and feeling His part in the sharing (more on this later).

Right now, I want to discuss some of the reasons we have difficulty establishing our communion with God and walking in all His promises to begin with. Here are a few of the reasons:

1. We don't know the promises.
2. We don't comprehend or trust (believe) the promises.
3. We don't recognize and counter the attacks of the enemy.
4. We don't take time to be still and know that He is God.

I listed number 1 first because it is the first critical step. It is also the easiest issue to fix, but it requires sustained effort on our parts. I can't stress how important it is for us to spend time reading God's Word every day. In Romans 12:2, Paul tells us:

> Do not be conformed to this world, but be transformed by the renewing of your mind, that by testing you may discern what is the will of God, what is good and acceptable and perfect.

So, how are we to renew our minds? We HAVE to read the Bible. Unless we are Jesus, who was born from heaven knowing God's will, or one of the prophets of old, or Paul to whom the will and Word of God was revealed ... AND WE ARE NOT ... we have to read to learn who God is, and who He says we are, and how we are supposed to live our lives. Despite our modern schedules, it is absolutely critical that we make time each day to read the Word. Many people believe that we should do this first thing in the morning ... to "start your day off right." While I tend to agree with their logic on the point, personally, I have found that doesn't work for me. I'm just not a morning person. I'm slow to wake up and until I have been up and stirring for a while, I just can't seem to clear the cobwebs enough to comprehend anything I try to read. However, I have found bedtime to be the hour that my mind seems to be the most troubled over circumstances in my life, stresses of the day, etc. So, what seems to work best for me is if I'll spend the last hour of my day reading my Bible. Doing so removes the clutter of the day from my mind and allows me to go to bed focused on what God says about me instead of what my circumstances tell me. I sleep better and wake up fully expecting God to be actively sorting out whatever is going on.

I do make it a practice to start my day off with a prayer (even if it is a groggy one) before I get out of bed in the morning. Doing so helps me to remember to look to God for strength throughout the day, instead of trying to muscle through everything on my own. It also opens the lines of communication between God and the Holy Spirit and me for the day before anything even has a chance to step between us. It's usually just a simple short prayer like, "Good morning, God. Thanks for another day. Help me remember to see and be grateful for whatever You plan to do for me today. Guide my steps and show me opportunities to glorify Your name as I walk through my day."

Number 2 on the list is an altogether different prospect. Reading the Bible versus understanding and trusting the promises of the Word are two totally different things. One can read the Bible and know what words it contains, but to renew our minds, we must take things a step further. We must actually understand and believe its words are true and applicable to us. Left to our own devices, this could never happen, but fortunately we are not left to handle the task alone. When we accept Christ as Savior, the third member of the Trinity, the Holy Spirit, is sent to dwell within our hearts. One of the Holy Spirit's many jobs is stated clearly in 1 Corinthians 2:12:

> Now we have received not the spirit of the world, but the Spirit who is from God, that we might understand the things freely given us by God.

How awesome is that?! God knows that broken humans could never understand His promises on our own, so He sends His Spirit to live inside believers to help them interpret and live in the words of the Bible. We have but to learn to tune in to the voice of the Spirit living inside us as we read the Word to know what to do. Sometimes reading a passage I've read many times, it is like a light suddenly comes on, and I see something new that I've never picked up on before. But more often than not, the revelation comes to me when I'm struggling in a particular situation, as described in the section above on dealing with my self-forgiveness issues. I don't know how many times I had previously read those three scriptures, but it was at least several. I had read them enough to know them, and I even understood their meaning. I just hadn't applied them to myself until in that moment of depression, I asked God why I was so troubled, why I kept having the same problem over and over. It was in that instant of humility that the Holy Spirit rushed those four verses to the surface in my memory, in the exact order I needed to see them to restore my peace. I couldn't tell you the chapter and verse, but I knew the promises. I understood them, and it was at that moment I realized they were included in the Bible FOR ME to call to mind and lean on for God's peace, working exactly as promised.

> Now faith is the assurance of things hoped for, the conviction of things not seen. (Hebrews 11:1)

So, how do we grow our faith? At first, we read the Bible to learn what God's promises are … and to see the illustrations of how they had been proven true by the narratives included throughout the Bible itself. The examples are awe-inspiring, to say the least! Our faith also grows from hearing stories from other believers who have walked through some of the same storms we might be facing. These are modern-day, firsthand accounts of God's words at work. From there, we can begin to claim the promises as our own and see that God delivers. He does indeed!

Again, as a reminder though, God is not a genie in a bottle granting all our wishes. Instead, He is the ultimately good Father. And just like when your kids tell you they want cake for supper, you will likely suggest they eat some real food first and then have cake for dessert, God is always looking out for our best interests. Likewise, when your children misbehave, your job is to correct them and show them the right things to do in life. God is the same way with us as His children. If we seek Him, He will lead and guide us to our best life. No promises it will be an easy life, but it will be blessed! Living under the promises of God really does provide a sense of peace that is beyond our human understanding (Philippians 4:7), regardless of the comfort or harshness of your surrounding circumstances.

Item number three on our list requires diligence on our part to pay careful attention to our surroundings as we watch for the enemy. Let's take a quick look at some scriptures about the devil:

> He was a murderer from the beginning, and does not stand in the truth, because there is not truth in him. When he lies, he speaks out of his own character, for he is a liar and the father of lies. (John 8:44, Actual quote from Jesus, Himself!)

> For even Satan disguises himself as an angel of light. (2 Corinthians 11:14)

> Be sober-minded; be watchful. Your adversary the devil prowls around like a lion, seeking someone to devour. (1 Peter 5:8)

Unfortunately, we are not on the lookout for a guy in a black cape with horns. Such would be easy enough, even for us, to spot quickly. We have to keep an eye on even the most harmless-looking scenarios and be vigilant in sorting out anything or any thought that is contrary to what we know God has told us in His Word. Paul says we have to take every thought captive to obey Christ (2 Corinthians 10:5). Even thoughts, especially thoughts, have to be monitored. Our thoughts are the devil's favorite playground. We are emotional creatures, and the devil knows it. Many days, all he has to do is catch us in a weak moment and whisper something into our subconscious, and we will pick it up and run with it … in the wrong direction. He loves reminding us of our past failures and sins (especially ones we have already confessed and been forgiven for), and then watching us beat ourselves up, feeling embarrassed about them. This is especially true if we carry it so far as to avoid praying or reading our Bibles because we feel too ashamed to approach God about these failures.

Here is the secret to avoid that trap: nothing you have done is ever hidden from God's eyes. He knows you did it. He knew you were going to do it, before the thought even crossed your mind. God loves you. He doesn't ever want you to hide from Him in shame. He wants you to bring it right up to His throne and say you're sorry so He can forgive you and remember it no more! Never hide in shame from God; that is when you need what He has to offer the most! The enemy comes to kill, steal, and destroy (John 10:10) ... but he has no power over us unless we give it to him (James 4:7-8).

On to number four. *Be still, and know that I am God* ... Psalm 46:10. Perhaps the sweetest words ever written when we learn how to use them.

Our fast-paced lifestyle does not aid us in this regard. The digital age and all of the technology we enjoy these days has destroyed the virtues that deferred gratification taught us just a generation ago. Cell phones with lightning-fast Wi-Fi and Google have us spoiled in our worldly life, with instant answers to every question or problem posed by man ... or so it would seem. The problem is that most Google answers come from man, and in the most serious issues of our time, man IS the problem, or the source of the problem.

God is more than capable of giving lightning-fast answers in time of need. Those stories are in your Bible, along with others. Parting the Red Sea (Exodus 14), fire from heaven (1 Kings 18; 2 Kings 1), and the account of Jesus calming the storm (Matthew 8; Mark 4; Luke 8) testify to this fact, as do all the miracles Jesus performed while He was on earth. But in our mortal, modern-day dealings, it is often more critical and beneficial for us to learn truths and lessons than it is to receive instant gratification from the prayers we offer.

God moves at His own pace, teaching us patience along the way. Sometimes this feels difficult to us, because we have a hard time slowing down enough to spend the quality time needed to develop our communion with Him. Our lifestyle and schedule have taught us to hurry up and get things done so we can receive the reward of our efforts, the praise of people, and the ability to move on to our next big project. That lifestyle is also the reason so many suffer from hypertension, stress disorders, depression, and heart disease. We are constantly in a rush; God is not. God is way more interested in seeing us growing in our faith and becoming more like Christ than simply dancing in deliverance.

Before we accept Christ as our Savior, God relentlessly pursues us through life's circumstances designed to nudge us toward Him. After we are saved, He relentlessly works life's circumstances to grow us in our faith, keep us on His path, and lead us to our best life. He truly is the Good Father. We don't deserve Him, and we fail Him every day; yet He is always right there with us.

Father, we thank You for never giving up Your pursuit of us. We are a stubborn people totally undeserving of the love, grace, and mercy You bestow upon us, much less the effort You exert in trying to deliver those good things to us. Father, open our eyes that we may see Who You are. Open our hearts that we may feel and receive Your gifts and teach us to be ever more grateful for the Giver rather than the gifts. Open the ears of our soul that we may hear the voice of Your Spirit, and give us the wisdom to shed our infantile, limited, worldly desires in favor of Your unlimited plan of blessing for us. Show us the smooth path You have made for us to walk, and show us Your pace that in our haste, we may not miss an opportunity to do Your bidding on our journey. In the mighty name of Christ we ask, AMEN.

---

[1] Google Dictionary. Accessed October 27, 2023. https://tinyurl.com/489bj56f.

6

WHAT WILL COMMUNION
WITH GOD BE LIKE?

THERE ARE A LOT MORE DETAILS I PLAN TO SHARE ON successfully fighting our daily battles, which enable us to stay on the path God has for us, but I want to pause for a moment to further illustrate exactly what it is we are seeking. I want to better define for us the GOAL of our spiritual walk. Let's face facts: if we don't know where we are trying to go, we certainly aren't likely to arrive on time, if at all; and if we don't truly recognize how wonderful the destination is, when the road becomes difficult, we are likely to back out of the trip and seek our pleasures and peace elsewhere. It is just human nature. So, with those thoughts in mind, I am going to attempt to paint a picture of what real communion with God looks like so that we are a hundred percent convinced that the destination is worth whatever amount of work we must put forth to finish the journey.

I gave the definition earlier that communion is the sharing or exchange of intimate thoughts and feelings, especially when the exchange is on a mental or spiritual level. From a human perspective, we know what a relationship of communion should look like with our spouse, our siblings, our families and our BFFs. Those are, or should be, the closest and most mutually beneficial human relationships in our lives. In good times or bad, we know those people we have in our lives who we can always depend on to have our backs when we need protection, to come to our aid when we need help, and to confront us to our faces when we need correction. As rewarding as those relationships can be, they pale in comparison to living in real communion with the God who created us and the universe we live in (Genesis 1) ... but what does that relationship look like? How does it work? And how can we establish it in our lives?

First of all, let's look briefly at how our closest human relationships are formed. Most children are born from their parents. We have a flesh-and-blood bond with them that began in our mother's womb, which strengthens and intensifies throughout our lives. In cases of children who are adopted, they may read this and think they are missing out on some critical aspect of familial bond, but I would argue that's not the case at all. If you happen to be adopted, the people you call parents basically loved you enough at first glance to go through the process of willingly rearranging their lives in exchange for being allowed to call you family. To me, that sounds like a bond at least as strong as blood, and I would encourage you not to discount your value to your parents, but to instead thank God that He put you in their path. Regardless of circumstance, through raising us, our parents nurture, love, teach, and correct us ... or at least they should.

Siblings share a very similar bond and need no further explanation or elaboration. BFFs, however, are slightly different. While a sibling could certainly end up in the BFF category, I'm talking more about those not-blood-related relationships in our lives. At some point in our lives, we meet them. Then over time, they proved themselves trustworthy, loyal, and loving. They may have made sacrifices of themselves for our benefit and certainly shared mutual love with us for a long period of time, and our bond with them grew and became stronger, year by year. The same is true for spousal relationships.

So with that understanding of how our closest human relationships of communion are formed, let's now look at how such a relationship with the Creator of the universe might work, beginning with some scriptural references:

> Then God said, "Let us make man in our image, after our likeness. And let them have dominion over the fish of the sea and over the birds of the heavens and over the livestock and over all the earth and over every creeping thing that creeps on the earth." So God created man in his own image, in the image of God he created him; male and female he created them. And God blessed them. And God said to them, "Be fruitful and multiply and fill the earth and subdue it, and have dominion

over the fish of the sea and over the birds of the heavens and over every living thing that moves on the earth." (Genesis 1:26-28)

For you formed my inward parts; you knitted me together in my mother's womb. I praise you, for I am fearfully and wonderfully made. Wonderful are your works; my soul knows it very well. My frame was not hidden from you, when I was being made in secret, intricately woven in the depths of the earth. Your eyes saw my unformed substance; in your book were written, every one of them, the days that were formed for me, when as yet there was none of them. How precious to me are your thoughts, O God! How vast is the sum of them! (Psalm 139:13-17)

For those whom he foreknew he also predestined to be conformed to the image of his Son, in order that he might be the firstborn among many brothers. And those whom he predestined he also called, and those whom he called he also justified, and those whom he justified he also glorified. What then shall we say to these things? If God is for us, who can be against us? He who did not spare his own Son but gave him up for us all, how will he not also with him graciously give us all things? (Romans 8:29-32)

For all who are led by the Spirit of God are sons of God. For you did not receive the spirit of slavery to fall back into fear, but you have received the Spirit of adoption as sons, by whom we cry, "Abba! Father!" The Spirit himself bears witness with our spirit that we are children of God, and if children, then heirs—heirs of God and fellow heirs with Christ, provided we suffer with him in order that we may also be glorified with him. (Romans 8:14-17)

There are a lot more scriptures we could look at, but these four passages have what I want to talk about covered, from before creation up to and including the point of our salvation and gift of the Holy Spirit. And that is the point in our lives where we become qualified to begin seeking our communion with God. They are pretty self-explanatory, but I want to touch each one to make sure we make the connection between them, and how our human relationships are formed.

Beginning in Genesis 1, God created us in His image ... that is, made us like Him, as opposed to all the other living beings in creation. Man is special and created to be in charge and above everything else living on Planet Earth. He was thinking about something special when He made us.

Psalm 139 says God knitted us together in our mother's womb, and we are fearfully and wonderfully made. Before we were made, every day of our lives had already been planned out and written down by God. Everything about us was known by God, before time began ... talk about forethought.

In Romans 8, Paul tells us that we are not Christians by our choice, but we were predestined by God for "sonship" before we were created. As Christians, we are adopted sons and daughters of God and joint heirs with Jesus.

Given these facts, look at the parallels against our human relationships of communion. Most of our closest human bonds are with our parents. God has been involved in our lives since eons before our parents were born. He created us in the womb (fearfully and wonderfully) and already knew every day of our lives before our parents, siblings, or friends ever met us. And He had already decided He was going to adopt us as His children prior to any of that taking place. He made us, knew everything about us, and planned out our amazing lives and afterlives before time began.

Are you beginning to be able to imagine how awesome a relationship of communion might be with a Father who loved you that much, and had given you that much thought before time began? I assure you, until you experience true communion with God, you haven't even the faintest clue of what real peace is yet. It just can't be imagined ... it must be experienced to be appreciated for what it is. The Bible gives us hints about it and lots of promises that are based upon it. But until we learn the meaning of asking, seeking, and knocking (Matthew 7:7-8), we won't understand how to walk in communion with God. We will get there, I promise, but it is a process. Bear with me; it's taken me years to get there, and I'm trying to condense what I have learned and seen work in my own life into a compact, decipherable few pages.

To lay the groundwork and foundation, I must go back to the scriptures. If I can't show it to you in the Bible, it isn't going to be correct! That statement is a life lesson that warrants a whole other book, because it is true of every aspect of life, but I digress. I am going to just throw these out there for now. We will discuss them later:

> Trust in the Lord with all your heart and lean not on your own understanding; in all your ways submit to Him, and He will make your paths straight. Do not be wise in your own eyes; fear the Lord and shun evil. This will bring health to your body and nourishment to your bones. (Proverbs 3:5-8)

> These things I have spoken to you while I am still with you. But the Helper, the Holy Spirit, whom the Father will send in my name, he will teach you all things and bring to your remembrance all that I have said to you. Peace I leave with you; my peace I give to you. Not as the world gives do I give to you. Let not your hearts be troubled, neither let them be afraid. (John 14:25-27, Jesus quote)

> I have said these things to you, that in me you may have peace. In the world you will have tribulation. But take heart; I have overcome the world. (John 16:33, Jesus quote)

> And we know that for those who love God all things work together for good, for those who are called according to his purpose. (Romans 8:28)

> Do not be anxious about anything, but in everything by prayer and supplication with thanksgiving let your requests be made known to God. And the peace of God, which surpasses all understanding, will guard your hearts and your minds in Christ Jesus. Finally, brothers, whatever is true, whatever is honorable, whatever is just, whatever is pure, whatever is lovely, whatever is commendable, if there is any excellence, if there is anything worthy of praise, think about these things. What you have learned and received and heard and seen in me—practice these things, and the God of peace will be with you. (Philippians 4:6-9)

> Not that I am speaking of being in need, for I have learned in whatever situation I am to be content. I know how to be

brought low, and I know how to abound. In any and every circumstance, I have learned the secret of facing plenty and hunger, abundance and need. I can do all things through him who strengthens me. (Philippians 4:11-13)

For we do not want you to be unaware, brothers, of the affliction we experienced in Asia. For we were so utterly burdened beyond our strength that we despaired of life itself. Indeed, we felt that we had received the sentence of death. But that was to make us rely not on ourselves but on God who raises the dead. He delivered us from such a deadly peril, and he will deliver us. On him we have set our hope that he will deliver us again. (2 Corinthians 1:8-10)

This is just a handful of the countless scriptures that give us insight into what we can expect to feel once we find true communion with God, and a few of the requirements for doing so. We will delve deeper into these, but just glance over the treasures in these verses personally. It's the secret of life. If you are not seeing it, peruse this little Q&A below:

How does one live a stress-free life? Lean not on your own understanding; don't worry about anything, but take everything to God in prayer and praise!

Where does peace come from? Fear the Lord and shun evil; believe the words of Jesus; focus on truth and the good things of God; learn to be content, whatever your circumstances!

How can we have hope in a hard life? Believe that God is in control and works ALL things (good and bad) for our good; don't rely on your own meager strength, but on that of the God who raises the dead! He has delivered us, and He will deliver us!!!

Knowing and believing these things are just a few of the benefits of walking in communion with the God of the universe! There are so many more, but picking up the peace that Jesus left for us and basking in it amid the chaos of the world we live in is certainly a blessing none of us deserve ... but God loves us so much that He sent Jesus to pay the penalty for our sins, just so that we could have it. Heaven is going to blow our minds! It is going to be so awesome; there are literally no words to describe it. But we do not have to wait until we die to get a taste of it. Once we learn to walk in communion with God, we get to live in the peace and promises right here in the middle of this fallen world! That, my friends, is what commun-ion with God is like!

Father God, flood us with Your Holy Spirit, and open our eyes so that we can begin to see the life You want for us here on earth. We know we are incapable of compre-hending the glory of heaven that awaits us, but we thank You for giving us Your promises to help us see mere glimpses of what we have to look forward to from right here, as we sojourn in this fallen land today. Open our ears to the voice of Your Spirit so that we may hear and feel Your words. Give us understanding so that we can ask and seek and knock until we find the key that opens the door to communion with You, and we thank You for it. In Jesus's mighty name, Amen.

7

STORIES OF COMMUNION, GRACE, AND PEACE

I N THE LAST CHAPTER, I TRIED TO PAINT A BROAD MURAL of what a blessing it is to be in communion with God. Now I want to show you a few examples from my own personal experiences of true communion just to give you a glimpse. Then I'll try to show you how to find it for yourselves. Every person is different from the rest, and every relationship is different as a result. I don't claim to know everything ... or much of anything outside my own life experience, but I would assume that since we are all different, communion with God would also be an original and unique experience for each individual. But I do believe that sharing my own personal experiences will be beneficial in showing you how amazing communion with God is and, hopefully, inspire you to diligently put forth the work required to experience it for yourself.

When we are able to find real communion, it's not uncommon to hear, or feel, the Holy Spirit speaking to us. It's not always an audible voice (though sometimes it is), but often just more of a feeling. Whether it is heard in an audible sense, or felt from somewhere deep inside you, it floods you with the most amazing sense of peace as it conveys the message to you. As I've walked through life, I have developed a habit of making notes for my-self of things that happen from time to time in which I see a deeper meaning than just the event itself. During times when I've done my part to walk in communion with God, I find these events of significance more prevalent in my life. The following are a couple such happenings I'd like to share as illustrations for you to read.

Little Things
June 18, 2019

I was cutting cedar today with a set of hydraulic snips on a bobcat. It was hot and dusty, but it's a job I rather enjoy because the roar of the engine, subdued by ear muffs, creates the perfect environment for pondering. As I get older, I find pondering to be more of a hobby of mine than it was in my younger days.

As I snipped and stacked the cedars, the wind was continually blowing dust in my eyes and debris all over me. More often than not, as I'd pick up the cuttings with the snips, limbs would break off, causing me to have to stop and get a new grip. These constant irritations were "harshing my mellow" and distracting me from my pondering.

I asked God, "Why must life be so filled with these little irritations?" And then followed that question with the thought, *God, I've learned to throw all my big dilemmas at Your feet and leave the outcome to You without fretting about them. So why am I constantly stressing over these insignificant, little irritations?*

I continued my pondering and my work, cursing under my breath each time I had to stop to re-grip or wipe the dust from my eyes; then, I'd pause my pondering to say, "Sorry God" each time I caught myself cursing. Finally, I became aware of and amused by this continuing cycle of events. I literally stopped and laughed at myself.

As I did so, I felt a sense of peace rush through my soul, and I remembered Psalm 46:10, "Be still and know that I am God!" I stopped my pondering and let my mind be quiet. I then started hearing a voice. It said, "Big trials of life are the easy part, because when circumstances in your life are too much for humans to handle on their own ... pretty much everyone turns and yields to God for help, even those who claim not to believe in Him!

"That stems from desperation and is not much of an indication of any significant level of faith. Remember Matthew 10:29-30?

"Are not two sparrows sold for a penny? And not one of them will fall to the ground apart from your Father. But even the hairs of your head are all numbered.

"Faith is just as important in dealing with life's little irritations as it is in dealing with the big trials. Nothing on your mind is too small for God to care about ... but humans seem to forget this and want to "handle" the little things on their own. This interrupts their walk and communion with Him ... then they wonder why they continue to get so bent out of shape over so many little, insignificant things.

"If you want to release your frustration over the little things, handle them the same way you do the big things ... give them over to God, as if they were big things. He's always right there beside you, waiting for you to look to Him instead of looking at your problems, even the little things.

"Little things, little, insignificant irritations of life, are nothing more than a gentle reminder to lean into the One who really cares."

Remember what I told you a couple chapters back of what 1 Corinthians 2:12 says is one of the jobs of the Holy Spirit?

Now we have received not the spirit of the world, but the Spirit who is from God, that we might understand the things freely given us by God.

When we establish communion in our daily walk, the Spirit is literally right there at our disposal to give us biblical wisdom, answer our questions, and interpret the promises of God to us as they relate to our current situation. It really happens just like that! Believe me when I tell you, there is nothing special about me. I'm as much of an average Joe/lay person as anyone who might ever read these words. I'm included with everyone else in the "all" of Romans 3:23's condemning: **"For ALL have sinned and fall short of the glory of God."** If I can find and walk in communion, and have this type of relationship and interaction with the Holy Spirit, anyone can. Here's another journal entry:

I had another "God moment" yesterday.
July 2, 2019

I finished up a five-day hunt on Monday, did my laundry, and came to Bandera because I needed to mow my yard and get my mail. It was about 9:30 p.m. when I finally got to the house, and I was exhausted. I went to bed about 10:15, and it was almost noon Tuesday when I woke up.

After my fourteen-hour hibernation, I was feeling groggy and hungry so I grabbed my gas jug and went to town to eat. Then I decided to go to Wal-Mart in Boerne for a few things and gas before getting all sweaty mowing. As I was driving to Boerne, I had K-LOVE on the radio and the song "Maybe it's OK" by We Are Messengers came on.

Two months ago, this song would send me into prayerful worship. Still recovering from the heartbreak of a painful divorce, tears would flow as I acknowledged my weakness (my "un-ok-ness") and threw it all at the foot of the cross, along with the mustard seed package of faith that God had begun to develop in me ... but today it was different.

As I sang the song, I recalled the emotions of sadness I used to feel welling up at the first note of the intro, but today they didn't come, and then it hit me. "I'm NOT, not ok any-more!!!"

How did this happen?! was my first thought.

Then I began to run through all the things that have taught me lessons over the last couple months: the devotion-als I've read, conversations I've had, the Bible passages I've read, the dust in my eyes, broken limbs, and cursing on the bobcat ... and a thousand other things that have somehow pointed me in the right direction for healing ... and I was just awestruck!

I exclaimed, "God!!! This is so amazing to me!! How do You use all these little things, the good and the bad and the hard...?" and I started listing the things I remembered.

But in the middle of my list, another voice began drown-ing mine out in my head. It said, "Why so astounded? You've read My promises. Are these questions you're asking, and the awe you are feeling, not exactly the fulfillment of those promises? Your one duty is to seek first the kingdom, so that all these things may be added unto you (Matthew 6:33), and now you are surprised that you have these things. The signs and wonders are right in front of you, every single day ... in all the good and in all the bad and the hard ... but if you aren't truly seeking, you don't notice them. That's why seek first is most important! If you fret first, or hurt first, or try to fix it on your own first, you miss the point. You have to give up your control ... because you are incapable on your own (John 15:5). There is no fear, or stress, or need to control in love (1 John 4:18) ...and God is love. Put down all the other stuff and just keep seeking."

That's where the peace and joy promised in the Bible comes from! None of my personal circumstances had changed. In the natural, I should still be miserable, lonely, and scared ... but I'm not! I'm ok, almost all the time now. And sometimes I'm even happy now and absolutely nothing has changed, except me. God is always the same, ALWAYS GOOD! So, whenever we can't feel Him or hear Him ... the problem definitely lies within us.

This was a huge revelation for me. I had been doing my best to "seek first the kingdom," but I wasn't sure I even really knew what that meant (we will talk more about this concept later), and I wasn't seeing any perceptible results, but I refused to give up. I just kept reading my Bible and trying to believe the promises; and then, out of nowhere, I was suddenly exactly where I was supposed to be, right where I had been the whole time, in the middle of the same circumstances ... but I was full of peace and joy! It IS amazing grace defined!

This last incident I'm about to share is a prayer that I wrote the day I was going to court to finalize a divorce I had fought for almost five years to avoid. Even though I knew I was doing the right thing, I was devastated; my heart was broken, and my spirit was crushed. I met with my attorney early that morning, and then he had a couple hours of work to do before the hearing was to begin. So I went into an IHOP to get some breakfast. I had no one else to talk to, so I pulled out my phone, opened up a new note, and just started typing a note to God. I didn't really have any words to say, but my soul just seemed to pour itself out into the note. It's obviously private and full of sorrow and pain, but I'm choosing to share it because in hindsight, I see it as a perfect example of a despairing person leaning into the promises of God.

Even though it was a sad day, when I finished typing, scrolled up, and began reading what my subconscious had written, I came to the amazing realization that the words somehow were God speaking to me, even more so than I had been speaking to Him. It was like communion auto-pilot. Tears flowed as I read it; they still do when I look back at it, but the tears were backed by a love and peace from God that made me see unequivocally that He was right there in the diner with His arm on my shoulder ... just like He promises to be ALWAYS, for every Christian.

Prayer Divorce Day

Good morning, God. As I'm sitting here staring at my coffee cup and facing the finality that this day is going to bring to this chapter of my life, I'm lost in a sea of emotions, as my human brain tries to wrap around all that's transpired and figure out what's next. You know the journey I've been on, and I want to thank You for continuing to love and pursue me until I finally got tired of running in the wrong direction. I never deserved that mercy, but none of us do. I guess that's the whole point of Your gospel of grace.

I know I don't need to tell You, because You already know, but I need to say the words just to get them out of my head so I can have some peace of mind. It's dark in my world today. I know You love me, and I know You have a good plan for me, and I know You work all things for the good of those who love You and are called according to Your purpose, but You also know there are times when we as humans can't feel any of that ... even though You put it all in black and white for us to read and lean into when we feel this way. Your message reminds us that You are all we need and that You provide whatever we need to be fruitful in whatever circumstance we find ourselves. We can see it in Your written Word, but we tend to lose the ability to feel it on the darkest days because our spirit is broken. When that happens, it's SO comforting to get the little reminders You lovingly throw in our direction, like the devos You brought to my attention last night, and the way "I Can Only Imagine" came on my radio the second I turned my truck on after visiting with my attorney this morning. God ... forgive my human inability to feel Your presence always with me, and please never stop hitting me in the face with those blatantly obvious reminders of Your love and mercy and grace: and grant me the wisdom to always recognize and appreciate them and their Source.

God, I don't even have a clue what's next for me. All I'm doing is trying to make it through this day, as I try to continually remind myself Who's I am and Who you say I am because honestly, I don't feel like I amount to much today. But I have this hope: the One who numbers my days has said He has a plan for me that is good, and I already know the day is coming when I will look back on all this and thank You that this hurt prepared me so well for whatever is coming next. When that day comes, give me the strength to sing that song to the world in such a way that will Hallow Your Name ... but for today ... just keep reminding me that You are right here with me, and that that is all I need.

In Jesus's *name... Amen.*

This prayer demonstrates every benefit of walking in communion with the God of the universe. Yes, it is sorrowful because I was sad when I wrote it, but if you look at the words, it's not just full of sadness and despair. It is chock-full of scriptures and biblical promises, some of which I didn't even realize I knew at the time. It is full of HOPE in the promises of God! In one of my biggest times of need, when I didn't even know what words I should say to ask for help, the Holy Spirit was pouring out the words for me, just like Paul told us he would in Romans 8:26-27:

> Likewise the Spirit helps us in our weakness. For we do not know what to pray for as we ought, but the Spirit himself intercedes for us with groanings too deep for words. And he who searches hearts knows what is the mind of the Spirit, because the Spirit intercedes for the saints according to the will of God.

This prayer shows the exact place all Christians should strive to live their lives, in good times and tough times ... but especially in hard times, because in our difficult times, we do not always think clearly. We need communion auto-pilot to step in and take over for us in those times. We need to throw out any false ideas of self-sufficiency in our good times, study our Bibles, and learn to lean on the strength of God in our everyday lives; so that in times of trial, it becomes second nature for us to lean into God and wait upon the direction of the Holy Spirit to lead us through the storms of life. In my prayer above, I thought I was talking to God. The reality is I was yielding to God, and the Holy Spirit was talking to me and showing me that I was not alone. I am not capable of praying like that on my own, even on a good day, much less when I am in despair. That was the promise of intercession from the Holy Spirit, alive and in action on my behalf. That is how our amazing God works!

Heavenly Father, we thank You that You have sent us Your Spirit to dwell within us to interpret Your promises and Your words to us; to show us how they actually apply to us in our daily lives and struggles; and to call them to the forefront in our minds when we need them the most. Father, thank You for loving us enough to desire communion with us and showing us through Your Word how we can learn to walk with You in such a special relationship. Open our hearts to see and understand this treasure for what it truly is, so that we will be inspired to seek it with all our hearts until we find Your place of peace. In Jesus's mighty name, we pray. Amen.

8

HOW EXACTLY CAN WE FIND THIS COMMUNION?

Then you will call upon me and come and pray to me, and I will hear you. You will seek me and find me, when you seek me with all your heart. I will be found by you, declares the Lord.

—Jeremiah 29:12-14

NOW THAT WE HAVE A VISION OF THE DESTINATION we are supposed to reach in our Christian lives, how exactly do we get there? The short, over-simplified answer is that we must learn, understand, trust, and apply the promises of God to every aspect of our lives, while putting on His armor and doing battle to kill the sin in our lives. That sounds simple enough, like something an attentive speed reader should be able to accomplish in a short time … if only that were the case.

Trust me when I tell you, it is an extremely short description of a task that will prove to require an unending, diligent daily effort on our part to achieve and maintain. We are so easily distracted; and over the course of our lives, to this point, we have developed so many bad habits we must fight to break in order to destroy and flatten the hills and roadblocks that we put up in front of ourselves on our journeys. Finding communion with God is not a sprint. It is a marathon … NO, it's a journey. That's the good news. The even better news is that if we truly seek this communion, God actually does all of the work. Our hurdle is that we have to learn how to get out of His way; and I must admit, that is much more of a daunting task than it seems at first glance as well.

So the first step toward communion (after accepting Christ as Savior) is learning the promises. The Bible is full of them, from front to back. Obviously that is going to take some time, just to read them all. Understanding them all requires much more time than just reading. Trusting them will develop through reading them in context and seeing the examples of them coming to fruition in the Bible itself, as well as hearing firsthand accounts of their truth from other believers. Learning to apply them to our own lives requires a joint effort from yourself and the Holy Spirit working from inside you.

That's a little longer, more detailed description of what we are up against. However, don't let it overwhelm you. Fortunately for us, it's a "play as you pay" kind of journey. In other words, we don't have to know everything, or do everything right to begin seeing God's work in our lives; we just have to start. And beginning to see the results as we venture into the journey definitely fuels our hunger for more and more of the same! Once we learn to recognize even the smallest, most mundane blessings we get every day, I promise you our excitement will build and give us strength and energy to dive in deeper and deeper. All we really have to muster is the strength to commit to starting the journey. As we learn to follow God, at His pace, He will literally take the wheel. Once we allow this to happen, our lives will never be the same again but in a good way.

Now, obviously in the context of this book, there is no way I can tell you all of God's promises, explain how they work, and tell you how to remember all of them. In the first place, I don't claim to know, understand, or remember them all. Secondly, my goal is not to pen the entire Bible. There is no need for that because it is already written; but I can tell you how I got started on my journey and share how I finally came to understand what it means to ask, seek, and knock (Matthew 7:7).

Once you've accepted Christ as your Savior, the first order of business is to learn who God really is; what He is like. The best way to do that is to begin in the New Testament and read the Gospels of Matthew, Mark, Luke and John. Those books tell the story of Jesus' life on earth; and Jesus shows us the essence of God. His life is the groundwork that everything else has to be built upon if it is to withstand the storms of life. Our human minds can't even fully comprehend the breadth and length and height and depth of love that Jesus showed for us (Ephesians 3:18). It is awe-inspiring and humbling, especially once our eyes are opened to how utterly undeserving we were before Christ. Even now, we are only deserving based on our faith in His merit. It really has nothing to do with us, and we can't get there on our own … ONLY through Jesus (John 14:6).

Once you've read the Gospels, then continue reading the rest of the New Testament. As you are reading, pay special attention to the scriptures that hold a promise and scriptures that define who you truly are in God's eyes. There are many, many such passages, and you will certainly not even recognize them all on the first time reading through. The Bible is literally alive with them. Even after you have read it a hundred times, you will continue to see new things that catch your attention, which you hadn't noticed before. Always, before you begin your daily reading, say a little prayer. Ask God to open your eyes so that you can see what He wants you to glean from your reading. He will always, ALWAYS answer that prayer! Even if nothing seems to jump out at you while you are reading, invariably, at some point in the future, you will have something happen that will cause you to remember something you might have read a month ago and see it in a new light. That is God and the Holy Spirit at work, and it's truly amazing when it happens. Those occurrences alone will help to begin building your faith, and it builds at an exponential rate!

In the paragraph above, I've alluded to a secondary, but extremely important, factor in your journey toward communion. In addition to getting to know who God is, and what He is like, it is equally important to learn who you are … in His eyes. I had not thought fully about this concept until I read another book on the subject titled, *Defined…Who God Says You Are,* and it is absolutely perspective-altering and life-changing. It's written by Stephen and Alex Kendrick and is based on the movie they produced, *Overcomer.* If you haven't read it, I can't recommend it enough. Finding true communion with God is difficult enough as it is. Fully understanding who we really are, as defined by God, gets us over the hurdle of unworthiness we naturally feel once we realize the expanse and enormity of good He promises to deliver to those of us who believe.

Sorry I got sidetracked there, but it was a noteworthy cul-de-sac. I'd recommend reading through the New Testament at least two, maybe three times before tackling the Old Testament. The Old Testament includes a ton of prophecies and symbolism that seemed to me much easier to read and understand after I was somewhat familiar with the New Testament. Once you know the New Testament stories, the Old Testament symbolism and prophesies come more to life and are easier to understand as you read them … at least they were for me. And it is important to become familiar with the Old Testament! It foreshadows the New Testament and the new covenant ushered in by the death and resurrection of Jesus. One can't truly appreciate the gift of the new covenant we get to live under before understanding all the requirements of the old covenant that preceded it.

Personally, I found it extremely beneficial when I purchased and started reading a Study Bible, instead of just reading the Bible itself. Study Bibles contain all the scripture, just like a regular Bible, but they also contain commentaries on the scriptures from biblical scholars, which help to explain and interpret passages. (It's like having your pastor handy to answer questions as you read.) So much of the wording and symbolism is difficult to grasp and understand due to language differences between the original manuscripts versus English, not to mention gaps between the old English language, from the time the Bible was originally translated into English, versus how we actually talk and think today.

Another note on that subject: there are many, many translations of the Bible available today. I haven't read them all. It is just my personal opinion, but here's why: I don't trust copies of copies of copies of copies! I'll be the first to admit that parts of the King James Bible are hard to understand in today's world. The English Standard Version is a lot easier to understand by regular people like me, and the wording of The Living Bible translation is much more like what we are accustomed to speaking and hearing in our modern times. I utilize those three versions. My study Bible is an ESV. My fear with the more modern Bible versions is that in their efforts to simply make the Bible more understandable to readers, there is the possibility that translators could interpret words from previously interpreted versions of previously interpreted versions in such a way as to change the meaning from that intended in the original texts. I'd like to think that diligence, ethics, and morals would prevent such errors from happening, but we are all human.

I'm just more comfortable working through my ESV Study Bible and its commentaries until I grasp the intended message from the original author of the text. As I get more knowledge and understanding of these texts, I will eventually read some of the "newer" versions, but at least by then, I'll hopefully have enough understanding of the "closer to original" texts to spot any inconsistencies, rather than potentially being misled by them.

On that note, I want to caution you regarding one other obstacle in finding true communion with God. There are LOTS of good churches led by great pastors all over the world. However, there are also a growing number of churches being taught false doctrines these days ... to the detriment of their congregations in particular, and society and Christianity in general. Whether this happens accidentally, through the pastors misinterpreting the meaning of the Scriptures, or intentionally, through the pastor intentionally misinterpreting the Scriptures to fit some hidden agenda (greed, popularity, etc.), the results are the same ... harm to the church. The so-called prosperity gospel being taught to so many these days is shameful, whatever the reason. God is not some genie in a bottle who can be summoned as needed to make us rich, grant us wishes, and/or give us a life of ease. While He is certainly capable, that is just not how He works. He is not interested in making our lives easy. He is interested in making us more like Christ.

God has a plan for each of us as individuals, and collectively as the body of Christ. It IS a good plan, and one that will certainly leave us blessed in this life. However, nowhere in the Bible are Christians promised an easy life, or a life of luxury, fame, or fortune. Instead, we are told that in this world we will face tribulation, but we are not to fear because Jesus has overcome the world (John 16:33), and we are also told that God will provide for all our needs (Philippians 4:19). If you find yourself being taught that Christianity is supposed to be all peaches and cream, it's time to find a new teacher. Real Christian life is indeed filled with peace, joy, and blessings. That is a fact, but the truth of the matter is that most of the time, our greatest lessons are learned in struggle, and our greatest blessings usually come to us through adversity. As Christians, our lighthouse beacon is Romans 8:28:

> And we know that for those who love God all things work together for good, for those who are called according to his purpose.

Ok. Sorry, I'm off that soapbox now. Let me show you the passage of scripture that was at first my biggest nemesis, until I finally figured out that it holds the key to walking in the life of communion with God that we are promised:

Do Not Be Anxious

Therefore I tell you, do not be anxious about your life, what you will eat or what you will drink, nor about your body, what you will put on. Is not life more than food, and the body more than clothing? Look at the birds of the air: they neither sow nor reap nor gather into barns, and yet your heavenly Father feeds them. Are you not of more value than they? And which of you by being anxious can add a single hour to his span of life? And why are you anxious about clothing? Consider the lilies of the field, how they grow: they neither toil nor spin, yet I tell you, even Solomon in all his glory was not arrayed like one of these. But if God so clothes the grass of the field, which today is alive and tomorrow is thrown into the oven, will he not much more clothe you, O you of little faith? Therefore do not be anxious, saying, 'What shall we eat?' or 'What shall we drink?' or 'What shall we wear?' For the Gentiles seek after all these things, and your heavenly Father knows that you need them all.

But seek first the kingdom of God and his righteousness, and all these things will be added to you.

Therefore do not be anxious about tomorrow, for tomorrow will be anxious for itself. Sufficient for the day is its own trouble. (Matthew 6:25-34, emphasis added)

WOW! That is a quote from Jesus, Himself, and folks, there is soooooo much packed inside those few short verses. I knew there was something special about that passage the first time I read it, but only after it all sunk in, and I began living my life by that mantra, did I fully recognize the bounty we have been given right there.

The portion I emphasized with italics should sound familiar. It was the answer that I quoted the Holy Spirit as giving me in my *I had another "God moment" yesterday* journal entry shared in the last chapter. I think that was the day the full weight of this scripture passage really hit me. Don't be anxious! Isn't life more than food and clothing? Am I not more valuable than the birds that God feeds every day? No amount of worry can add a single hour to my life! Heathens worry about stuff like this, but God knows we need all these things ... it's the secret of life! And it's so simple, yet we don't understand it. We don't trust it. We don't apply it to our own lives, and we make things so hard:

> *Seek first the kingdom and his righteousness...*and *all* these things *will be added* to you. (Matthew 6:33, emphasis added)

Friends, that is a promise directly from the mouth of Jesus. We can never find a more reliable source for truth and information than that! Remember earlier when I told you that I'm convinced lots of people believe IN God, but very few actually just BELIEVE God? This is where the rubber hits the road. If you want real communion with the God of the universe, then you absolutely must learn to BELIEVE His words. As fallen humans, sojourning in a cursed world, we are unaccustomed to trusting anyone, or anything, a hundred percent. That is one of those bad habits I mentioned, which we have to break. We are still sojourning in a cursed world, but if we have accepted Christ as our Savior, we have been given a new heart and a new identity in Christ. This is why it is so important to strive to learn who God is, what He is like, and who He says we are. Once we wrap our minds around those things, we can learn it IS safe to actually believe God. In fact, believing God is the only thing in this life that is a hundred percent failsafe! It is the secret to finding and walking in communion with Him and living our best life.

If you are a new Christian, don't fret; your faith will begin to grow as you learn more about who God is and who He says you are now, in Christ. As I learned, that scripture passage contains the essence of the whole message of this book. However, it took me some time and labor to figure that out. I began my journey, exactly as I have suggested you do, by just starting to read, but if I can hit some of the highlights for you as you are starting your journey, perhaps you can learn from my missteps and get to your destination quicker than I did. I pray it's so, but I wouldn't trade a single second, or avoid a single trial, from my own walk for anything. The journey really is that awesome!

Here is another related passage that frustrated me to no end as I began trying to plant my feet on God's intended path for me. It is another quote from Jesus in the very next chapter of Matthew.

Ask, and It Will Be Given

> Ask, and it will be given to you; seek, and you will find;
> knock, and it will be opened to you. For everyone who asks
> receives, and the one who seeks finds, and to the one who
> knocks it will be opened. Or which one of you, if his son asks
> him for bread, will give him a stone? Or if he asks for a fish,
> will give him a serpent? If you then, who are evil, know how
> to give good gifts to your children, how much more will your
> Father who is in heaven give good things to those who ask
> him! (Matthew 7:7-11)

Now, keep in mind that this passage is only seven verses past the one
I just quoted. That being the case, the word "seek" struck a chord of emphasis in my mind as "ask" and "knock" expounded on the concept. I knew
I was looking for something, something desirable that I didn't feel I had …
and I knew it was important. My problem was I couldn't put the concept
together in my feeble mind for the longest time. I believed in Jesus, but I
hadn't yet wrapped my mind around the idea that there was a difference
in believing in versus simply believing Jesus. I read these texts over and
over. I even prayed about them, but I seemed to get no answer (because I
hadn't yet learned how to BE STILL), and I just continued to wrestle with
the concept in my mind, trying to understand and figure it out. I very much
liked what it said, "Ask, and it will be given; seek, and you will find; knock,
and it will be opened to you." Sounds so simple … and who wouldn't want
that, right?

I figured asking was praying … seemed logical enough. I was reading
my Bible, and that was the only way I could think of to seek … was I missing something? And I just had no idea what I was supposed to knock on.
Like I said, it frustrated me to no end for quite some time, until one day
when I was talking to a friend. It was just a normal conversation, about life
and such. My friend was going through a tough time that wasn't dissimilar
from something I had been through and overcome in the recent past, and
as we talked, I suddenly became very aware that I was quoting scriptures
… and the longer we talked, the more scriptures I quoted just in the course
of a normal, everyday conversation. It wasn't like I was "preaching" or anything. I'm not even sure if at the time, he knew or recognized that I was
quoting scriptures throughout our talk, but it certainly caught my attention

and got me thinking. As our conversation wound down, we shared a prayer. He thanked me for the advice and said it helped him feel better.

After we parted company, I sat down for a bit trying to figure out where all those scriptures I heard myself sharing had come from. I realized that as I was going through that particular trial myself, I had read those scriptures. Then, I recognized that they must have meant more to me at the time than I realized. At that time, I was simply "reading my Bible and doing my homework," just trying to learn the things I am encouraging you to do as you begin your journey toward communion with God. I was actually just "seeking" by reading and trying to see for myself who God was. Nobody had told me to pay particular attention to anything that I saw as containing a promise or who God said I was, but obviously my subconscious had been doing just that; otherwise, my mind wouldn't have hung onto those things I had just heard myself sharing with my buddy. It was then that it hit me: those scriptures had, in fact, helped me get through the trial I was going through. Unbeknownst to me, God had been working to heal me and help me WHILE I was "seeking." I had also been praying about my situation during that time ("asking") and had received my answer in the form of being helped to overcome my trial. When I acknowledged these things, my faith began to grow. That's how it works. That's how the promises work. I said a little prayer of thanks after coming to this realization.

While I was sitting there as this revelation sunk in, a couple more scriptures suddenly surfaced in my mind:

> These things I have spoken to you while I am still with you. But the Helper, the Holy Spirit, whom the Father will send in my name, he will teach you all things and bring to your remembrance all that I have said to you. (John 14:25-26; that's a Jesus quote)

...and Paul said:

> Blessed be the God and Father of our Lord Jesus Christ, the Father of mercies and God of all comfort, who comforts us in all our affliction, so that we may be able to comfort those who are in any affliction, with the comfort with which we ourselves are comforted by God. For as we share abundantly in Christ's sufferings, so through Christ we share abundantly in comfort too. (2 Corinthians 1:3-5)

Why did those two passages come to mind? I'm no biblical scholar, but I truly believe it was because I was just BEING STILL and knowing He was God (Psalm 46:10). It has been my experience that when I "be still" and know that He is God, it quiets my mind. When our mind is quiet, we can literally hear or feel the Holy Spirit talking to us. That's when we can learn. Not only had God helped me when I wasn't even cognizant of it, the words of Jesus and Paul were proven true and reliable, along with the scriptures I had quoted to my buddy in the process.

I hadn't intentionally, or even consciously made any effort to memorize those scriptures I heard myself quoting that day, but obviously the Holy Spirit had grabbed them as I read and etched them into my heart as they healed me. All I had done that day was stop what I was doing so I could lend an ear to a buddy in need. I was willing ... and the Spirit reminded me from deep inside my heart where my peace and comfort had come from, so I could share it with someone else who needed it. As I pondered these things, quietly, the Spirit took the opportunity to teach me another lesson and show me more TRUTH from the scriptures. That is the beginnings of communion. We can't see it or understand it until we see it and understand it... That might not make sense right now, but I promise it will when it happens to you.

I wanted communion and I knew it was missing, but I didn't know how to get it. So, I just started reading and vowed to keep reading and studying until I got it! I had felt frustrated because I couldn't understand how asking, seeking, and knocking worked, right up to the point where I realized that it had been working the whole time, beginning the second I started reading my Bible. I still had much to learn, but from that day forward, I have never questioned those passages again. If I can't see those promises working in my life every single day, I know there is a problem with me that I need to fix. God is the same every day ... ALWAYS there with me, ALWAYS being good and loving me, and ALWAYS keeping His promises one hundred percent of the time. It will work exactly the same way for you.

Our Father in heaven, hallowed be Your name. Thank You for sending Jesus to provide us this gateway, through which we are allowed to boldly approach Your throne, and thank You for Your Word that shows us the way to You. Teach us patience and perseverance as we begin to ask, seek, and knock in our search to walk in communion with You. Grow our faith, Father, as we strive to learn of Your faithfulness. We ask that the Holy Spirit illuminates the scriptures to us as we read so that we can truly see Your love that backs the promises in Your Word. Teach us to BE STILL ... and know that You are God. Quiet our minds and open our ears to the voice of Your Spirit. Give us eyes to see that You are our greatest treasure, and the only source of value we will ever find in this life. We praise You and thank You for being the same merciful and loving Father to us yesterday, today, and forever. In Jesus's name. Amen.

9

WHAT ELSE DO
WE NEED TO KNOW?

Even though we rest in Jesus for a part of our salvation, we shall fail if
we trust to self for anything. No chain is stronger than its weakest
link: if Jesus be our hope for everything, except one thing, we shall ut-
terly fail, because in that one point we shall come to nought.

—Charles Spurgeon[1]

THAT LINE FROM CHARLES SPURGEON IN HIS BOOK, *ALL*
of Grace, shook the foundation of my soul and defined the importance of walking in this communion with God in our lives. I
think the reason it had such a profound impact upon me is likely because I
spent several decades prior to reading it "trusting to self" instead of "rest-
ing in Jesus" and, as alluded to earlier, my outcome had not been very desirable. I spent most of my life proving Spurgeon's (and the Bible's) words
true. Read it again:

> Even though we rest in Jesus for a part of our salvation,
> we shall fail if we trust to self for anything.
> No chain is stronger than its weakest link:
> if Jesus be our hope for everything,
> except one thing,

we shall utterly fail,
because in that one point we shall come to nought.

Spurgeon didn't originate that thought and concept. He simply expounded upon the words of Jesus in John 15:5; *"apart from me you can do nothing."*

Nothing…

What are we capable of under our own strength in this life?

Nothing!

When we are having good luck and success in our careers, our families, and/or our daily lives, and we think it is owed to our diligence, our hard work, our good deeds … read that verse again. Read that Spurgeon quote again. Folks, I assure you, it ain't us.

When Jesus said, *"apart from me you can do nothing,"* He was stating a fact and giving us a warning of truth. Here is some biblical support:

> Every good gift and every perfect gift is from above, coming down from the Father of lights. (James 1:17)

All good things that come to us are gifts of God's grace, *every good gift* … period! Success in our families, jobs, and daily lives are gifts from God. If you are performing well at some aspect of life and being rewarded for it, it is because God created you to have the abilities and arranged the circumstances in order such as to make you successful. Don't try to take credit for your work. Thank God for giving you the talents to get the job done. Why? Because apart from Him, you can do *nothing*!!! And if you don't believe that statement is true … if you think you can handle your own life and you don't need God to help you every single day, life will eventually demonstrate the truth of that fact for you. I spent a lot of years of my life living contrary to this philosophy before life finally humbled me, to the point that I had nowhere else to turn. When I did turn, I found that God was right there waiting for me just as promised.

God has a plan for us … and it is good (Jeremiah 29:11). He is good. He loves us, gives us everything we need to be fruitful for His purpose and full of joy (John 15:11) … and all He desires, in return, is for us to love and follow Him into *our* best life.

Our life is a series of events and trials designed to draw us to Him. He wants a relationship with each of us … but He gives us free will to choose how we live our lives. We have free will, but He still desires a relationship with us because before He created us, He designed our best life paths as the one we would choose to walk with Him. Apart from Him, we cannot be living our best life. He loves us and knows what's best for us, and we just don't!

When we choose to ignore His call for relationship and ignore His blessings that are designed to draw us to Him, then life becomes a series of events and trials designed to push us to Him. He doesn't give up on us ... ever! Life is hard ... but it's even harder when we use our free will to make the wrong choices and decide to try to live our lives under our own strength, refusing to accept and be grateful for God's blessings and help. We can't do it on our own. Life is just too heavy for us. We need God, and He is always there for us, waiting for us to figure out that we can't do it without Him.

After a four-year-long struggle with depression and loneliness, I finally came to a remarkable realization: even though I had "given my troubles to God," I had failed to release my grip on them as I had placed them in His hand. Yes, I had learned to trust God ... sort of, and I had "practiced growing my faith" ... sort of, and I had been "diligently seeking God's will and plan for my life" ... sort of. My revelation was that I was still doing all the above on my own terms. Yes, I was sincere in my search ... but I was keeping limits on both my search and my spiritual growth by subjecting them to my own timeline. I wanted to hurry up and be better. I wanted to see results by such-and-such time. I was trying to put God in a box, but He doesn't work on our timeline. He does everything in His perfect timing. (More about this later.)

I've learned that my timeline and my limited human understanding stymie the growth of faith. I'd spend countless hours reading my Bible, searching for MY answers in earnest, but when I'd finish reading for the evening, I'd find myself amazed by the stories of victory from the apostles ... and dismayed by my own continued "losses." I was feeling depressed and doubting God's goodness because after I put down my Bible and turned out my light to go to bed, I found myself still surrounded by loneliness.

The funny thing about this in hindsight is that one of my favorite scripture passages is 2 Corinthians 12:7-10:

> So to keep me from becoming conceited because of the surpassing greatness of the revelations, a thorn was given me in the flesh, a messenger of Satan to harass me, to keep me from

becoming conceited. Three times I pleaded with the Lord about this, that it should leave me. But he said to me, "My grace is sufficient for you, for my power is made perfect in weakness." Therefore I will boast all the more gladly of my weaknesses, so that the power of Christ may rest upon me. For the sake of Christ, then, I am content with weaknesses, insults, hardships, persecutions, and calamities. For when I am weak, then I am strong.

The truth that finally jumped out of this and smacked me in the face was nobody knows for sure what Paul's "thorn in the side" actually was ... and I now think that is because it just doesn't matter. I believe that IS the cornerstone secret behind his message in that brief passage of scripture. Here's the key: we all have a thorn in our side, or we have had one, or, at some point, we all will have one. When it happens, Paul's message is our key to dealing with it: do not allow the thorn to consume and devour your whole existence. That creates loneliness, depression, anxiety, and misery. As Christians, that is not who we are supposed to be. I believe that Paul's message is that it makes no difference what our problem, or issue, or difficulty, or our "thorn" is. When we recognize it, pray about it, and then know that God has our request (1 John 5:15). He will deal with it according to His supreme will and good plan, and use it to get us to where He wants us to be. God is good. His plans are good. We know and are assured that: ALL things work together for good for those who love the Lord (Romans 8:28).

Believe me! I know it's easier said than done ... but, just like Paul, after you pray about it, proceed on forward with your life, just loving the Lord. Don't do like I did for four years and let yourself doubt the goodness of God, or think that God is holding a grudge against you for some sin you have already repented of. Sometimes God just answers us with a "No" or a "not yet." When He does so, it is for our own good (Romans 8:28). I don't fully understand why my answer was no. Maybe it was like Paul, to keep me from becoming conceited again like I once was. But I do know this: God is good! His plans are good. And all things work together for MY good, because I love the Lord. If I can just yield my wants and desires, and my timeline, to His will and pace, my life will be blessed and full of peace and joy. Since I figured that out, I've had a new peace descend upon me that I had never experienced in my life.

If you want to have a happy life, you cannot let your past define you. When you don't forgive, you hold anger and resentment inside you, or you question God's goodness and presence in your life: you just can't be happy. Your attitude, demeanor, and perceptions are shaped by what you have inside you. So if you have unforgiveness, anger, or any of these negative human emotions that you are carrying around from your past, that is the definition of letting your past define you. You can't see and appreciate the good of today because you are perpetually blinded by the baggage of your past. Forgive and pray. Let go of that baggage. Never let your own emotions define you. Ask God to help you let go and heal from the hurts of your past and the pains of your present. Ask God to shape and mold you into who He made you to be. Read and listen to His Word, and let God define who you are. Then, constantly remind yourself and the enemy who God says you are. That is how you find rest and peace in your life.

There are times in our lives when we can't feel God's presence nearby, and that's ok because our faith isn't based on our feelings. Our faith is based on our hope, and we hope for what we can't see or feel.

> Now Faith is the assurance of things hoped for, the conviction of things not seen. (Hebrews 11:1)

The key to remembering this is to ALWAYS remind ourselves that in times when we can't feel God near us, the problem lies within us, not Him. He has promised to never leave or forsake us, (Isaiah 41:10; Hebrews 13:5), and we know His Word is true. So, when we can't feel Him close, we need to look inward for whatever is blocking His presence in our lives. It could be any number of things, such as unforgiveness in our hearts toward someone who wronged us—or even toward ourselves, unconfessed sin, doubt, fear, frustration, anger, self-pity, or any of our other skewed human emotional states. God knows that we are fickle, broken humans, living in a fallen world. He understands how much harm it does us when we allow our emotions to control our mindsets and demeanors, instead of allowing our faith in His promises to guide our thinking and our actions. That is why He wants us to walk in communion with Him. If we are walking in communion with Him, He will be our guiding influence in everything we do and every thought we have. His presence eliminates the torturous effects of all our trials in life, if we will just yield to Him and His will for us.

How does He do that ... eliminate the torturous effects of all our trials in life? He gives us instructions, hope, and the promises of His Word to learn, understand, and apply to our own lives, like this:

For I consider that the sufferings of this present time are not worth comparing with the glory that is to be revealed to us. For the creation waits with eager longing for the revealing of the sons of God. For the creation was subjected to futility, not willingly, but because of him who subjected it, in hope that the creation itself will be set free from its bondage to corruption and obtain the freedom of the glory of the children of God. For we know that the whole creation has been groaning together in the pains of childbirth until now. And not only the creation, but we ourselves, who have the firstfruits of the Spirit, groan inwardly as we wait eagerly for adoption as sons, the redemption of our bodies. For in this hope we were saved. Now hope that is seen is not hope. For who hopes for what he sees? But if we hope for what we do not see, we wait for it with patience.

Likewise the Spirit helps us in our weakness. For we do not know what to pray for as we ought, but the Spirit himself intercedes for us with groanings too deep for words. And he who searches hearts knows what is the mind of the Spirit, because the Spirit intercedes for the saints according to the will of God. And we know that for those who love God all things work together for good, for those who are called according to his purpose. For those whom he foreknew he also predestined to be conformed to the image of his Son, in order that he might be the firstborn among many brothers. And those whom he predestined he also called, and those whom he called he also justified, and those whom he justified he also glorified.

What then shall we say to these things? If God is for us, who can be against us? He who did not spare his own Son but gave him up for us all, how will he not also with him graciously give us all things? Who shall bring any charge against God's elect? It is God who justifies. Who is to condemn? Christ Jesus is the one who died—more than that, who was raised—who is at the right hand of God, who indeed is interceding for us. Who shall separate us from the love of Christ? Shall tribulation, or distress, or persecution, or famine, or nakedness, or danger, or sword? As it is written,

"For your sake we are being killed all the day long; we are regarded as sheep to be slaughtered."

No, in all these things we are more than conquerors through him who loved us. For I am sure that neither death nor life, nor angels nor rulers, nor things present nor things to come, nor powers, nor height nor depth, nor anything else in all creation, will be able to separate us from the love of God in Christ Jesus our Lord. (Romans 8:18-39)

This passage was written by the apostle Paul. Paul wasn't having financial problems, or job issues, or marriage problems, or any of the type problems we face now in modern-day life. Paul was being literally persecuted for his beliefs and for preaching the Gospel of Jesus Christ. He was arrested, imprisoned, beaten with rods thirty-nine times, as well as stoned and left for dead. Paul had REAL life-and-death problems, which he faced daily … just because he refused to stop telling people about Jesus. Yet instead of feeling sorry for himself, or doubting God's promises, he uses his words to encourage us in our menial modern struggles: trying to pay bills, dealing with being passed over for a promotion, or getting over someone saying something that hurt our feelings.

He tells us the sufferings of this present time are not worth comparing with the glory that is to be revealed to us; the Spirit helps us in our weakness; if God is for us, who can be against us; in all these things we are more than conquerors through him who loved us; and I am sure that neither death nor life, nor angels nor rulers, nor things present nor things to come, nor powers, nor height nor depth, nor anything else in all creation will be able to separate us from the love of God in Christ Jesus, our Lord.

If he can say these words in the midst of persecutions, such as imprisonment, beatings, and literally being stoned to death, can we not find comfort in them in our own significantly less dire circumstances? Oh, to find even a small portion of the faith in God's promises that filled the apostle Paul. He is a role model second only to Jesus.

Father, we come to You in praise and worship, for You are worthy. We are seeking You with all our hearts because Your Word tells us that is how we find You. God, You know how hard it is for our human minds to understand and apply Your promises to our lives. Though we try and fail daily to live our lives in a manner pleasing to You, we thank You that Your mercies and grace come to us fresh and new, with every dawn, to renew our strength as we battle to renew our minds in

Your Word. Father, we know Your promise to never leave us or forsake us is true, but You know that our limited human vision doesn't always allow us to feel You, even though You are always right here beside us. Open our eyes, Lord, so that we may begin to see Your hand in everything as we walk through our days in search of You. Give us the awareness to recognize the work of Your hands, especially in the little things, and the wisdom to be grateful for Your blessings and help. We ask in the mighty name of Jesus, Amen.

---

[1] Charles Spurgeon, *All of Grace* (New Kensington: Whitaker House, 2002).

10

HILLS, HURDLES, ROADBLOCKS, AND THE ENEMY

S O, WHAT HAVE WE LEARNED ABOUT SEEKING COMMUN-
ion so far? All we have to do is learn and understand the promises of
God, trust them, and apply them to every aspect of our lives. Doesn't
sound all that difficult ... right? If that were the whole story, we would be
looking at smooth sailing on this journey ... but we haven't talked about
the obstacles yet. And, like I told you a few chapters back, if I can't show it
to you in the scripture, it isn't going to be correct. So, let's take a look at a
couple references here:

Peace with God Through Faith

Therefore, since we have been justified by faith, we have
peace with God through our Lord Jesus Christ. Through him
we have also obtained access by faith into this grace in which
we stand, and we rejoice in hope of the glory of God. Not only
that, but we rejoice in our sufferings, knowing that suffering
produces endurance, and endurance produces character, and
character produces hope, and hope does not put us to shame,
because God's love has been poured into our hearts through
the Holy Spirit who has been given to us. (Romans 5:1-5)

Testing of Your Faith

> Count it all joy, my brothers, when you meet trials of various kinds, for you know that the testing of your faith produces steadfastness. And let steadfastness have its full effect, that you may be perfect and complete, lacking in nothing.
>
> If any of you lacks wisdom, let him ask God, who gives generously to all without reproach, and it will be given him. But let him ask in faith, with no doubting, for the one who doubts is like a wave of the sea that is driven and tossed by the wind. For that person must not suppose that he will receive anything from the Lord; he is a double-minded man, unstable in all his ways. (James 1:2-8)

Now we know Jesus already told us in John 16:33, *"in this world you will face tribulation, but fear not for I have overcome the world."* So the fact that we will face obstacles is no surprise. But here, Paul and James are taking this concept a step further for us. We are to "rejoice in our sufferings" and "count it all joy" when we get to face these obstacles of life because as Christians, we are guaranteed by Romans 8:28 that ALL things work together for good for us. Now we can begin to understand how this is possible! Suffering produces endurance. Endurance produces character. Character produces hope. Trials test our faith and produces steadfastness. We can be assured that when we walk through our obstacles in communion with God, we will always come out better, smarter, and stronger on the backside. And remember 2 Corinthians 1:3-5 from further back in the book?

> Blessed be the God and Father of our Lord Jesus Christ, the Father of mercies and God of all comfort, who comforts us in all our affliction, so that we may be able to comfort those who are in any affliction, with the comfort with which we ourselves are comforted by God. For as we share abundantly in Christ's sufferings, so through Christ we share abundantly in comfort too.

Not only are we strengthened by going through our trials in communion with God, at the same time, we are being better equipped for His service. As Christians, we are the church and the body of Christ. One of our jobs in the kingdom is to help our brothers and sisters in Christ. When we have been through a trial in communion, we come out the other side with a never-ending well of comfort to share with others who might be facing things we have already conquered. I can testify firsthand that nothing gives meaning and value to suffering that we have been through as much as using what you learned to help someone else who is struggling. Once you see this in your own life, you will quickly realize that in walking through life's obstacles in communion with God, we are strengthened, comforted, equipped, and *blessed*. That's why, and how, we can count it all joy!

Yes, there are obstacles. In fact, our journey is pretty much guaranteed to be an obstacle course for most of the trip, but hey, God isn't looking for a bunch of weak, half-hearted Christians. He wants us to be warriors for Christ, and the best way to get strong is to eat right and exercise. So, we feast on the Word of God and exercise our faith on the obstacle course of life. It is both a fulfilling and rewarding endeavor. I promise that until you have helped someone overcome a struggle that you yourself have walked through, you have never experienced true Christian joy!

With that preface, let's talk about some of the obstacles we can expect to face in our journey of communion. For me, it is easier to discuss these by breaking them up into categories. I just made this up because it makes sense to me. Hopefully it will be easy to understand for everyone. Here are the categories I came up with and a brief indicator of how I defined them:

1. Hills—self-made obstacles

2. Hurdles—obstacles formed from our bad habits and strongholds.

3. Roadblocks—sometimes God closes doors.

4. The enemy—be vigilant against falling prey to his schemes and lies.

HILLS

The first obstacle types I want to address are the hills in our lives. As I've already explained, hills are not external obstacles but are issues that block our communion with the Father, stemming from our wrong mindsets. By our very nature, we like to feel that we can control our environments, and that we are in control of our own destinies. The simple truth of the matter is that we can't, and we are very much not.

Pride is defined by Webster's Dictionary as "inordinate self-esteem: conceit."[1] Whether we want to admit it or not, pride is the reason humans feel the need to control; and we all have it in our lives ... some more so than others, but *all* humans have it in their lives ... and it is a sin. It is also a source of the hills in our lives. The Bible warns us repeatedly of this fact:

The fear of the Lord is hatred of evil. Pride and arrogance and the way of evil and perverted speech I hate. Proverbs 8:13

By insolence comes nothing but strife, but with those who take advice is wisdom. Proverbs 13:10

Pride goes before destruction, and a haughty spirit before a fall. Proverbs 16:18

For who sees anything different in you? What do you have that you did not receive? If then you received it, why do you boast as if you did not receive it? 1 Corinthians 4:7

Therefore let anyone who thinks that he stands take heed lest he fall. 1 Corinthians 10:12

These are just a few of the warnings about pride in our lives. There are many, many others throughout the Bible, because pride and how we handle it is a *huge* determining factor in the amount of peace and joy, or lack thereof, in our lives. The reason is simple. As our pride grows, it shifts our focus from God and His goodness onto ourselves. If we are going to walk in communion with God, He has to be the center of our lives. If He is the center of our lives, we can trust His promises, and this allows Him to be in control of our thoughts, emotions, and actions.

On the contrary, as pride moves us toward the center of our own existence, we find ourselves grasping to control all aspects of our lives, which pushes God from the central focus. Without God as our center, we lose our gift of Jesus's peace as we begin more and more to see our surrounding circumstances. This causes our emotions to panic and fret and torment us with questions and thoughts, such as, *How can this possibly work out? How am I going to get out of this mess? What am I gonna do now? This is too big for me to face! I can't do this anymore...* Sound familiar? I can show you this issue in the Bible as well. Check it out:

Jesus Calms a Storm

On that day, when evening had come, he said to them, "Let us go across to the other side." And leaving the crowd, they took him with them in the boat, just as he was. And other boats were with him. And a great windstorm arose, and the waves were breaking into the boat, so that the boat was already filling. But he was in the stern, asleep on the cushion. And they woke him and said to him, "Teacher, do you not care that we are perishing?" And he awoke and rebuked the wind and said to the sea, "Peace! Be still!" And the wind ceased, and there was a great calm. He said to them, "Why are you so afraid? Have you still no faith?" And they were filled with great fear and said to one another, "Who then is this, that even the wind and the sea obey him?" (Mark 4:35-41)

The disciples were literally in the boat *with* Jesus, yet they panicked. They had seen the things Jesus was capable of, and He had explained to them who He was and what He was on earth to do ... but they still didn't understand. Jesus *did* understand! He was in such a place of peace and rest in the promises of God that He would have literally slept through the entire, stormy trip, knowing God was going to get Him where He was supposed to be had the panicked disciples not awakened Him. I have two thoughts on this story:

1. I want the peace in my life that Jesus had in His ... and I know it is available to me because He told me so in John 14:27 when He said, *"Peace I leave with you; my peace I give to you. Not as the world gives do I give to you. Let not your hearts be troubled, neither let them be afraid."* This is promised to us, and the only way we can have it is if we walk in true communion with God, on His terms, and at His pace, just like Jesus did!

2. The disciples, who were literally hanging out *with* Jesus every day, eventually did get this peace, but in order to do so, even they had to learn to trust the promises ... and they were seeing them fulfilled on a daily basis.

Now we don't physically get to hang out with Jesus, but He has promised to never leave us or forsake us (Hebrews 13:5). And, while we don't literally get to see Jesus walking on water, calming the storms, healing the sick, and raising the dead, that does not mean we are expected to just trust blindly in a bunch of things we can't see. Even though He isn't still here on earth in bodily form, God is still in control, and the work of His hands is still visible. We just have to yield to His will and stop trying to forge our own paths. If we can learn to understand, trust, and apply His promises, instead of trying to control our own lives, we CAN SEE Him working in our lives every single day!

Still on pride, there is a godly form of pride that is not a sin. It actually builds us up as Christians.

> In God we have boasted continually, and we will give thanks to your name forever. Psalm 44:8

> But far be it from me to boast except in the cross of our Lord Jesus Christ, by which the world has been crucified to me, and I to the world. Galatians 6:14

> But God chose what is foolish in the world to shame the wise; God chose what is weak in the world to shame the strong; God chose what is low and despised in the world, even things that are not, to bring to nothing things that are, so that no human being might boast in the presence of God. And because of him you are in Christ Jesus, who became to us wisdom from God, righteousness and sanctification and redemption, so that, as it is written, "Let the one who boasts, boast in the Lord." 1 Corinthians 1:27-31

Remembering scriptures such as these helps us to keep our focus on God, and God at the center of our lives. Always keep in mind the Spurgeon quote and "trust nothing to self." Three things create the hills in our lives: 1. Not knowing the promises of God; 2. Not understanding the promises of God and applying them to our lives; and 3. Pride–self-sufficiency. Work hard at keeping God as the center of your life, and many of your hills will disappear before you reach them on your journey. *"In all your ways acknowledge him, and he will make straight your paths"* (Proverbs 3:6). If you don't enjoy exercising on the obstacle course, heed this proverb so God can flatten the road for you!

HURDLES

Hurdles and hills are related in that both are created by our faulty mind-sets, misperceptions, and habits. The difference between the two is that while hills are created from ignorance, disbelief, and pride, hurdles and strongholds stem from false beliefs, doubt, fear, and bad habits.

> Humble yourselves, therefore, under the mighty hand of God so that at the proper time he may exalt you, casting all your anxieties on him, because he cares for you. Be sober-minded; be watchful. Your adversary the devil prowls around like a roaring lion, seeking someone to devour. Resist him, firm in your faith, knowing that the same kinds of suffering are being experienced by your brotherhood throughout the world. (1 Peter 5:6-9)

In moments of weakness, we can be completely paralyzed by doubt and fear. Like a lion hunting prey, the enemy can smell fear a mile away. And such paralysis is exactly the opportunity the enemy is ever watchful for because it is the perfect time for him to whisper half-truths and outright lies in our ears. If we are not overly vigilant in our efforts to recognize and combat this tactic, it can be very easy for us to take these false thoughts and hold them tightly as truth. This allows the enemy to cause us to form negative strongholds in our minds (God must be mad at me. I'm too far gone for God to care about. God could never love me after what I've done … etc.). Negative strongholds cause us to form bad habits in our lives based on lies from the enemy. Once formed, breaking down these strongholds requires a lot of work through the renewing of our minds by studying the Word of God (Romans 12:2).

> For though we walk in the flesh, we are not waging war according to the flesh. For the weapons of our warfare are not of the flesh but have divine power to destroy strongholds. We destroy arguments and every lofty opinion raised against the

knowledge of God, and take every thought captive to obey Christ. (2 Corinthians 10:3-5)

A stronghold is defined as "a place that has been fortified so as to protect it against attack" or "a place where a particular cause or belief is strongly defended or upheld."[2] In our minds, we form strongholds with certain beliefs all throughout the course of our lives. Now if we spent our entire life in the earnest effort of renewing our minds (Romans 12:2) by reading God's Word, this would be awesome; but we all know this has not been the case. Therefore, it is important that we assess each of these fortified beliefs and check their validity when placed alongside everything we read in our Bibles. The enemy (father of lies, as per John 8:44) has been whispering lies and half-truths to us our entire lives. It is very likely that over the course of the time we spent not walking in communion with God, we have adopted and fortified in our minds some of these falsehoods; that is just what the devil does. So, it is critical that as we read our Bibles, any time we read something that seems contrary to what we have been believing, we scrub the lie, destroy the stronghold, and replace it with God's truth. That is how we break strongholds (2 Corinthians 10:4)!!!

There is no fear in love, but perfect love casts out fear. For fear has to do with punishment, and whoever fears has not been perfected in love. (1 John 4:18)

A good test for our beliefs we have stashed in stronghold fortresses in our minds is to assess if quoting the statement creates in us a sense of peace and calm, or fear and anxiety. Then compare this answer with 1 John 4:18, which tells us, "There is NO fear in love." God is love; and there is no fear in love. So if a certain belief in our mind creates a sense of fear or anxiety in our emotions, that belief needs to be deleted and overwritten with scripture because it is not from God; and it is holding us back from our best life.

Once we take this step and destroy these strongholds in our minds, we must be on the lookout for any habits we might have formed in our daily lives based upon them. If our fears and anxieties cause us to avoid certain things, topics, or aspects of life, look to the Bible for how to break down these barriers. More likely than not, some of our greatest blessings lie hidden behind that which we feared for the wrong reasons. God just seems to work things that way to enable our spiritual growth and make us more Christlike.

ROADBLOCKS

There are times in our journeys toward communion with God that our lives will seemingly come to a standstill; at least it has been the case for me on many occasions. It seems to happen most often to me immediately after I had seen a new revelation of some sort. I'll delve into this topic more fully in a bit, but I wanted to touch on it here in this chapter on the obstacles we can expect to face on our journeys. I refer to these times of standstill as roadblocks.

Sometimes God just closes doors that we really think we need to walk through to get to the next level of our journeys. When these times come, God has a reason. He doesn't do anything randomly, even though at the time, it may seem so to us in our limited human understanding. Sometimes the door is permanently closed because we aren't supposed to walk through it at all, and other times God is simply slowing us down to His perfect pace, because we are not yet ready for what awaits us on the other side of that threshold. In times of running into such a roadblock (or any of the obstacles mentioned), my initial reaction is most often to beat my head against the wall in frustration … because I am a hardheaded moron … lol. Cycling through this so many times in my life, however, has taught me unequivocally that patience is indeed a virtue. This lesson is much easier grasped if we can just learn to STAY in communion and listen carefully for the voice of the Holy Spirit, as we encounter each and every obstacle.

How does one manage this feat of wisdom and strength, you ask? We stay in communion by exactly the same means as we get into communion with God. Learn, trust, and apply the promises of God … in particular for this case, Jeremiah 29:11 and Romans 8:28; and keep God at the center of our focus. Despite our frustration and lack of understanding, we simply have to continue to remind ourselves that: 1. God is good; 2. God is in control; 3 God has a good plan for us; 4. God works everything for our good; and 5. He loves to teach us patience! The first few verses of Psalm 75 is a good read any time we hit a roadblock:

> We give thanks to you, O God; we give thanks, for your name is near. We recount your wondrous deeds. "At the set time that I appoint I will judge with equity. When the earth totters, and all its inhabitants, it is I who keep steady its pillars. I say to the boastful, 'Do not boast,' and to the wicked, 'Do not lift

up your horn; do not lift up your horn on high, or speak with haughty neck.'" (Psalm 75:1-5)

"At the set time that I appoint I will judge with equity...it is I who keep steady its pillars." God is good! His plan for us is good! His timing is *always* perfect! Trust these things and listen to the Holy Spirit at every obstacle!

THE ENEMY

Nothing irritates the devil more than a Christian who has learned, trusted, and applied the promises of God to their lives. That person is living in absolute peace, all day/every day, no matter what life throws at them. The devil hates anyone who finds truth and peace in God's Word and will stop at nothing to get them off track! That being the case, it is a sure bet that any time we encounter an obstacle, as we are walking in communion with God, the enemy will immediately swarm us and begin spewing lies. He doesn't care who or what he lies about. He will use anything and everything he can think of to get our focus off of God. It's just who he is and what he does.

When we are truly seeking first the kingdom and the life that God designed for us, Satan knows his best opportunity to derail us and get us to stumble off the path God has made smooth for us is in times when we run into obstacles. He obviously can't break our focus off of God when we are being blessed and singing praises, but if he can catch us in a moment of frustration or doubt, as we are being faced with some trial of life, he will jump at the chance to whisper lies in our ears. From the dawn of creation, this has been his favorite tactic. One has to look no further than Genesis 3:

> Now the serpent was more crafty than any other beast of the field that the Lord God had made. He said to the woman, "Did God actually say, 'You shall not eat of any tree in the garden'?" And the woman said to the serpent, "We may eat of the fruit of the trees in the garden, but God said, 'You shall not eat of the fruit of the tree that is in the midst of the garden, neither shall you touch it, lest you die.'" But the serpent said to the woman, "You will not surely die. For God knows that when you eat of it your eyes will be opened, and you will be like God, knowing good and evil." So when the woman saw

that the tree was good for food, and that it was a delight to the eyes, and that the tree was to be desired to make one wise, she took of its fruit and ate, and she also gave some to her husband who was with her, and he ate. Then the eyes of both were opened, and they knew that they were naked. And they sewed fig leaves together and made themselves loincloths. (Genesis 3:1-7)

This account appears in the very beginning of the third chapter of the very first book of the Bible ... talk about the oldest trick in the book! It's almost like people just couldn't wait to mess things up for themselves, but let's hold off on any harsh judgement for a moment because if we don't, it will come back around and bite us right on our posterior gluteus maximus.

Instead, let's take a closer look at what really happened here and the consequences.

Adam and Eve were placed by God right smack in the middle of paradise. They had everything they could ever want, living in the most beautiful place in the world. And to make it even better, they had real and literal communion with God. Every day, He would come and walk around and hang out with them in the Garden of Eden. They couldn't possibly have a better life. Those were the circumstances of their existence!

So on this particular day, they're out for a walk when Eve meets this talking serpent, who mixes a lie with a half-truth. Now pay close attention to what really happened here next: "*So when the woman saw that the tree was good for food, and that it was a delight to the eyes, and that the tree was to be desired to make one wise...*" Keep in mind, this woman lived in paradise, in actual communion with God: yet she suddenly felt the need to be wise? That's the Bible's words for what happened. My interpretation is that Eve suddenly had a rise in pride, and it caused a hill to pop up in her life...

Remember in our discussion of the hills, the three things that create the hills in our lives: 1. Not knowing the promises of God; 2. Not understanding the promises of God and applying them to our lives; and 3. Pride—self-sufficiency. Adam and Eve knew and understood the promises of God because He had laid it all out for them when He placed them in the garden. Her problem was she now suddenly craved self-sufficiency. She wanted to be wise. She wanted to be like God and know the difference between good and evil. She wanted to be in control. Pride created the hill in Eve's life; and it was the undoing of communion with God by all normal people, all the way up until the point that Jesus came and made a way for us to once again be allowed as individuals to approach God under the new covenant of grace.

So, they ate the apple, realized they were naked, and hid from God. That is the effect of any sin in our lives. It makes us ashamed and causes us to feel the need to hide from God. If you read the rest of that story, it is easy enough to see that trying to hide from God, or trying to hide our sin from God, is a futile endeavor. It serves only to break our communion with God and make us miserable. Don't do it!

The New Life

Now this I say and testify in the Lord, that you must no longer walk as the Gentiles do, in the futility of their minds. They are darkened in their understanding, alienated from the life of God because of the ignorance that is in them, due to their hardness of heart. They have become callous and have given themselves up to sensuality, greedy to practice every kind of impurity. But that is not the way you learned Christ! — assuming that you have heard about him and were taught in him, as the truth is in Jesus, to put off your old self, which belongs to your former manner of life and is corrupt through deceitful desires, and to be renewed in the spirit of your minds, and to put on the new self, created after the likeness of God in true righteousness and holiness.

Therefore, having put away falsehood, let each one of you speak the truth with his neighbor, for we are members one of another. Be angry and do not sin; do not let the sun go down on your anger, and give no opportunity to the devil. Let the thief no longer steal, but rather let him labor, doing honest work with his own hands, so that he may have something to share with anyone in need. Let no corrupting talk come out of your mouths, but only such as is good for building up, as fits the occasion, that it may give grace to those who hear. And do not grieve the Holy Spirit of God, by whom you were sealed for the day of redemption. Let all bitterness and wrath and anger and clamor and slander be put away from you, along with all malice. Be kind to one another, tenderhearted, forgiving one another, as God in Christ forgave you. (Ephesians 4:17-32)

Sin grieves the Holy Spirit, which causes the sense of guilt and shame that we feel. If left unchecked, this causes us, like Adam and Eve, to try to avoid God's presence because we feel unworthy. Work to kill the sin in your life (Romans 8:13); and when you do sin, *never* run or hide from God when you mess up. Everyone messes up. It's a guarantee, and it will happen on a daily basis. *"For all have sinned and fall short of the glory of God"* (Romans 3:23, emphasis added). Don't let it break your communion. When you realize you have messed up, run *to* God in repentance so He can forgive you and remember it no more (Hebrews 8:12) and get you back onto the path He has made smooth.

Finding communion and walking your best God-designed path requires diligence, real effort, and commitment on your part. Once you successfully find it, more diligence, real effort, and commitment is required to keep it. Satan's number one goal is to prevent you from finding communion with God to begin with. His number two goal is to trip you up and cause you to fall out of communion with God when you have been successful at finding it. That is why when life is good and things are going smoothly for us, it is so critical to trash the idea of self-sufficiency and pride for the garbage it is; instead, we should practice praising God for the blessings we are receiving. Do it so much that it becomes your initial reaction to everything good that happens. That way, when you find yourself in a crisis, your initial reaction will already be to look toward God, instead of looking at your circumstances and to yourself. Remember the Spurgeon quote: "…trust to self for nothing!"

The devil doesn't give much thought to mediocre, self-sufficient, muddling-through-life Christians. They are miserable enough on their own and don't have time to do much damage to his worldly kingdom. It is those of us who really reach for all the promises entitled to us through the blood of Jesus, and who are willing to do the things God has called us to do in His service, that pique the devil's interest and receive the most of his attention and efforts. If you do not feel like you are battling Satan on a daily basis, you probably aren't living your best life and should get deeper into your Bible and step up your game!

Heavenly Father, we thank You and praise You for the wisdom of Your words. Make us ever hungry for more. Illuminate the promises so that our eyes can see and our hearts can understand. Father, teach us to embrace the trials and obstacles of life for the lessons and treasures they provide; and remind us that all we need do is lean on You and Your word as we face them. Use them as only You can to make us stronger, wiser, and more like Christ. Help us learn to keep You at the center of our lives. Expand our awareness so that we never miss an opportunity to share Your love and comfort with those around us. We praise You for it, and we thank You for it in the precious name of Jesus. Amen.

---

[1] Websters Dictionary 1828, October 27, 2023, webstersdictionary1828.com/Dictionary/pride.

[2] Google Dictionary. Accessed October 27, 2023. https://tinyurl.com/7ycv3en2.

11

KEEPING IT ONCE YOU FIND IT

Y OU KNOW HOW WHEN YOU GRADUATE FROM HIGH school or college, you get a diploma attesting that you have completed the requirements for graduation that you can frame and display on your wall forever? Or when you excel at some sport and win a trophy, that memento stays with you always on display to remind you of your victories? Well, finding and achieving true communion with God is nothing like either of those things. Sorry to burst your bubble there ... but I've already alluded to this fact in some of the previous chapters.

Diplomas and trophies are things we can "earn" as humans. The communion we are seeking with God is a free gift to us, earned and warranted solely by our faith in the blood and sacrifice of Jesus. We can't buy it, and we certainly can't earn it. Remember Romans 3:23? As sinful humans in a fallen world, the only thing we are capable of earning on our own merit from God is His just and wrathful judgement of eternal damnation in hell ... but for Jesus.

> Jesus said to him, *"I am the way, and the truth, and the life. No one comes to the Father except through me."* (John 14:6, emphasis added)

Only because of Jesus are we able to be adopted as sons and daughters, afforded the means by which we may approach the throne of God in prayer, and allowed the opportunity to receive the benefits of the blessings and walk in the promises of God in communion with Him. All these things are promised to us for free through our faith in Jesus … and that is the only means by which we can have these free gifts. Since we can't earn these things, we have no reason or right to expect that once we find the peace Jesus gives us in John 14:27, we should just have the diploma or trophy to stick up on a shelf in our home for the rest of our lives. It's not a prize; it is the treasure of a journey … a never-ending journey that walks us through our best possible life!

That peace, the same peace that allowed Jesus to sleep through the storm that had the apostles stressed to their wits' end, is truly the ultimate treasure that this life has to offer! Finding it and keeping it should be our ultimate goal, and I promise you it is worth whatever amount of effort required for us to seek it out. That is the definition of *"seek first the kingdom"* because if we do this, *"all these things will be added to us"* (Matthew 6:33)!

We have learned that to find communion with God, we have to learn the promises from the Bible, trust the promises, and apply them to every aspect of our lives. But once we have done that, how do we then keep the communion alive in our lives? The best answer I can give is to continue seeking. The Bible isn't just a book that we can read like all other books and then assume we know what is in it. The Bible is the Living Word of God!

> For the word of God is living and active, sharper than any two-edged sword, piercing to the division of soul and of spirit, of joints and of marrow, and discerning the thoughts and intentions of the heart. And no creature is hidden from his sight, but all are naked and exposed to the eyes of him to whom we must give account.
>
> Since then we have a great high priest who has passed through the heavens, Jesus, the Son of God, let us hold fast our confession. For we do not have a high priest who is unable to sympathize with our weaknesses, but one who in every respect has been tempted as we are, yet without sin. Let us then with confidence draw near to the throne of grace, that we may receive mercy and find grace to help in time of need.
> (Hebrews 4:12-16)

Jesus came and lived life as a human on earth. He was tempted in every way and dealt with our struggles in life just like us; only He did it without sin, and without forgetting to live in peace under the promises of God. The more we read the Bible, the more we learn, though we can never know all it contains. We can never know and understand all the promises, but through prayerful study (seeking first the kingdom), we can rest assured that the Holy Spirit will continually reveal to us all that we need to know, day by day, to ensure we are able to live our best life ... the life that God designed for us to walk.

> The steadfast love of the Lord never ceases; his mercies never come to an end; they are new every morning; great is your faithfulness. (Lamentations 3:22-23)

God's mercies and grace toward us are never-ending. He throws us whatever we need, fresh and new every morning; we just have to remember to look for the package. As long as we keep seeking, we will keep finding! However, it is important to remember that it is not just us seeking that we must do to stay in communion with God, once we successfully find it. We still have our sinful human nature, hills, hurdles, and the enemy to contend with, not to mention whatever other tasks and responsibilities life dictates we are responsible for at the same time. Looking at the overall picture can be a bit overwhelming and disheartening through our natural eyes; but fortunately, in the process of seeking first the kingdom, God takes care of all that for us. If we work to keep Him at the center of our lives, He teaches us to view our lives through His lens instead of our human lens.

There are literally scriptural secrets and promises that allow us to deal with any circumstance that life, or the enemy, throws at us from the security of peace that Jesus promised us in John 14:27. It takes some study, prayer, and active seeking to get there, but Paul outlined the secret of how to deal with all of the above in his letter to the Ephesians:

The Whole Armor of God

> Finally, be strong in the Lord and in the strength of his might. Put on the whole armor of God, that you may be able to stand against the schemes of the devil. For we do not wrestle against flesh and blood, but against the rulers, against the authorities, against the cosmic powers over this present darkness, against the spiritual forces of evil in the heavenly places. Therefore take up the whole armor of God, that you may be able to withstand in the evil day, and having done all, to stand firm. Stand therefore, having fastened on the belt of truth, and having put

on the breastplate of righteousness, and, as shoes for your feet, having put on the readiness given by the gospel of peace. In all circumstances take up the shield of faith, with which you can extinguish all the flaming darts of the evil one; and take the helmet of salvation, and the sword of the Spirit, which is the word of God, praying at all times in the Spirit, with all prayer and supplication. To that end, keep alert with all perseverance, making supplication for all the saints, and also for me, that words may be given to me in opening my mouth boldly to proclaim the mystery of the gospel, for which I am an ambassador in chains, that I may declare it boldly, as I ought to speak. (Ephesians 6:10-20)

Let us sort through the symbolism there:

- *having fastened on the belt of truth*—The truth is God's Word, the very promises that we must seek to learn, understand, and trust so that we can apply them to our lives.

- *having put on the breastplate of righteousness*—We are counted as righteous due solely to our faith in Jesus, and the sacrifice He made so that we could receive forgiveness of our sins.

- *as shoes for your feet, having put on the readiness given by the gospel of peace*—This is why we must seek first the kingdom. Learning to walk in communion with God is the only way we can really find and walk in the peace that Jesus promised to give us.

- *take up the shield of faith*—Faith is the key to everything as a Christian. It is the only means by which we receive salvation. It is the only means by which we can walk in communion. It is the only way we can resist the schemes of the enemy. We absolutely have to believe God! I read a short devotion recently that contained a quote saying, "The steps of faith Fall on the seeming void, and find The Rock beneath."[1] I must apologize for failing to note the author. I will note that those beautiful words do not belong to me, but I was moved by them, and they stuck with me. No truer words have never been spoken.

- *take the helmet of salvation, and the sword of the Spirit*—We are secure in our salvation. The Spirit within us testifies to the fact that we are children of God (Romans 8:16). He teaches and leads us into the life God designed for us, and He prays for us and through us.

- *praying at all times in the Spirit*—Prayer is so critical in our lives; it is our lifeline. I always start my day with, "Good morning, God" before I even get out of bed. My last words before going to sleep are usually, "Good night, God" and all through the day, I talk to Him … like a friend. I'm quite sure there are times when others think I am talking to myself, and I'm ok with that. The comfort we get from knowing that God is always right there beside us, willing to hear our thoughts, is worth a few strange looks from others.

Understanding all these things and making a practice of applying them to our lives really does help lighten our daily load to a manageable level, even in times of trial. And the tougher the trial, the more time we should spend each day searching the Bible for answers, talking to God about our concerns, and listening for guidance from the Holy Spirit.

The simple fact of the matter is that just because you do the work required and achieve communion with God, it does not mean from that point on you will always have communion with God. Due to ongoing sin in our lives, attacks from the enemy, and our natural human tendency toward trying to do things our way, it is almost a certainty that even when we are consciously trying to stay in communion with God, we will still find ourselves outside its boundary from time to time. Remember my pastor's analogy of driving in the dark and fog on a winding Hill Country road? When you feel like you've lost the communion, don't panic. Just get back to the basics of searching your Bible for the particular promise that you need; pray and ask the Holy Spirit for help; and then listen while being still and knowing He is God! Put off your plans and your will to get in step with His, and your life just can't get any better.

Father, we thank You that Your mercies are new every morning. As we walk through our journey seeking communion with You, we ask that You open our hearts to see the value of the treasure that is You and Your peace. Fuel our hunger for it and make our need for You so readily apparent to us that we learn to forsake all the things of this world to pursue more of You. Shield us from the obstacles that threaten to cause us to stumble, Father; and as we approach each obstacle, open our ears to hear the voice of Your spirit guiding us through on Your perfect path. Blind our eyes to the distractions of our circumstances and surroundings so that we aren't inclined to take our focus off You. Strengthen us as we battle the sinful nature of our human bodies and give us endurance and steadfastness in this fight. Forgive us for our failures and remind us when we fail to always run TO You in repentance. Teach us to yield to Your mighty hand, as You mold and make us more like Christ. We ask these things and praise You for them in the mighty name of Jesus. Amen.

---

[1] QuoteFancy. Accessed October 27, 2023.
https://quotefancy.com/quote/1468497/John-Greenleaf-Whittier-Nothing-be-fore-nothing-behind-The-steps-of-faith-Fall-on-the.

12

How Does Prayer Factor In?

PRAYER ... WHAT AN AMAZING GIFT IT IS! THANKS IN total to the work of Jesus, we as adopted children of God are afforded the ability to walk right up to the throne and speak directly to our awesome God. He loves us immensely ... *no*, that's too small a word. He loves us *infinitely*! He is never not with us, never asleep, or too busy to listen to us: and He doesn't even care what we want to talk about. He just wants us to talk to Him because He adores us.

No problem is too big or too small. No question or concern is too complicated or too insignificant for Him to give us His undivided attention. He wants us to have the peace that Jesus left for us in John 14:27, even if it means we need Him to be available to us 24/7, 365. He doesn't lend us an ear begrudgingly; instead, He always welcomes us like a loving father listening to his child relating their story of a major life event. He just can't wait for us to come talk to Him because that is how He knows we value Him. That is who our God is.

> And this is the confidence that we have toward him, that if we ask anything according to his will he hears us. And if we know that he hears us in whatever we ask, we know that we have the requests that we have asked of him. (1 John 5:14-15)

> Rejoice always, pray without ceasing, give thanks in all circumstances; for this is the will of God in Christ Jesus for you. (1 Thessalonians 5:16-18)

Is anyone among you suffering? Let him pray. Is anyone cheerful? Let him sing praise. (James 5:13)

"Watch and pray that you may not enter into temptation. The spirit indeed is willing, but the flesh is weak." (Matthew 26:41)

Rejoice in hope, be patient in tribulation, be constant in prayer. (Romans 12:12)

These are just a handful of the countless scriptures dealing with prayer that are included in our Bibles. When it comes to walking in communion with God, prayer factors in! God isn't looking for polished professional pray-ers ... Yes, I just made that word up, but it is truth. God wants us to be at ease talking to Him. He expects our reverence, because He truly deserves it. But His goal is to bring us into communion with Him so that we can see the reality of the truth of His promises and be able to walk in the peace that Jesus promised us. He knows we can't ever have that if we are timid or bashful about approaching and talking to Him.

If praying is a "new thing" for you, don't overthink it, and don't try to "impress" God with lengthy, well-scripted prayers. Just talk to God like you would talk to a friend. Tell Him what is on your mind. Tell Him how your day went. Tell Him about your concerns. Ask Him to help you to know what to do so that you can get to where He wants you to be. Thank Him for the good things you have in your life, while asking Him to make you more aware of the little things He does for you every day. Then remember to thank Him for all those things. Pray for your friends and ask God to do the same things for them that you are asking for yourself. Praying isn't hard, and it doesn't need to be "fancy" to be effective. How do I know this? I paid particular attention to a quote from Jesus:

And they were bringing children to him that he might touch them, and the disciples rebuked them. But when Jesus saw it, he was indignant and said to them, "Let the children come to me; do not hinder them, for to such belongs the kingdom of God. Truly, I say to you, whoever does not receive the kingdom of God like a child shall not enter it." (Mark 10:13-15)

...and Paul:

But I, brothers, could not address you as spiritual people, but as people of the flesh, as infants in Christ. I fed you with milk, not solid food, for you were not ready for it.
(1 Corinthians 3:1-2)

...and Peter:

Like newborn infants, long for the pure spiritual milk, that by it you may grow up into salvation — if indeed you have tasted that the Lord is good. (1 Peter 2:2-3)

When we accept Jesus as Savior, we are born again. God removes our hearts of stone and give us new hearts of flesh, putting His Spirit within us (Ezekiel 36:26-27). Newborn Christians need a steady diet of spiritual milk so that we can grow into mature Christians. We are saved immediately, but growing into who God designed us to be is a process. Just like the growth and maturity of children, it begins with a sense of awe and wonder at every aspect of our new world, the character of God, and the bounty and truth of all His promises as we grow to understand more and more of them. Part of the maturity process is becoming aware and in awe of the power of prayer as a gift of God. God knows (and now you do too) that we learn how to pray in baby steps. No genuine prayer is insignificant to our God, even if it is spoken in the words of a child ... or a spiritual child. There is no shame in learning ... at any level. Talk to God, especially if you think you aren't very "good at it"! You will get better, but you won't ever get any more effective if you are sincere and speak in faith.

Here's another Paul quote to keep in mind as you learn about prayer:

Now to him who is able to do far more abundantly than all that we ask or think, according to the power at work within us, to him be glory in the church and in Christ Jesus through- out all generations, forever and ever. Amen.
(Ephesians 3:20-21)

God hears and answers *all* of our prayers, and He always does more for us than we can even think to ask. His answer could be yes, or no, or not yet. I've found thus far in my journey that some of my biggest blessings have been prayers that God answered with a "*no*"; and even when the an- swer is yes, it may not manifest in the form that we had in mind as we made the request. Never forget, God is the ultimately good Father. He has a good plan … *the best plan* … for us, and His best plan doesn't always line up with our plan for ourselves. In fact, it almost never does, because unlike Him, we truly have no idea what is good for us, much less what is BEST for us. Learn to yield your human wants and will to His. You will be grateful you did.

If you ask God to give you more faith, or to make you more like Christ, or to bless you in some way (and you should ask for all these things daily), don't be surprised or discouraged if you find yourself in a trial or test of faith shortly thereafter. When you learn to lean on God as the center of your world, nothing grows your faith as much, or as fast, as facing a life situation that you can't control so you must totally rely on God to get you through it. Nothing can make you more like Christ than being refined in the fires of life. And your biggest blessings will usually come on the backside of conquering obstacles by trusting in God's promises, seeing them work in your life firsthand, and then sharing those experiences with others. Such things are what produces the peace that Jesus promised us and causes it to manifest in our lives. When you learn these things and learn to let God work through you, instead of trying to handle things in your own strength, you will begin to humbly and automatically expect God to take care of any obstacles you incur. Stepping into communion with God is the secret to eliminating stress, worry, and anxiety from your life and replacing them with faith, peace, and joy.

> Do not be anxious about anything, but in everything by prayer and supplication with thanksgiving let your requests be made known to God. And the peace of God, which surpasses all understanding, will guard your hearts and your minds in Christ Jesus. (Philippians 4:6-7)

> Likewise the Spirit helps us in our weakness. For we do not know what to pray for as we ought, but the Spirit himself intercedes for us with groanings too deep for words. And he who searches hearts knows what is the mind of the Spirit, because the Spirit intercedes for the saints according to the will of God. (Romans 8:26-27)

Philippians 4:6-7 is one of my favorite passages of scripture in the whole Bible! It serves to remind us how to avoid stress and anxiety in our daily lives, telling us quite clearly, and in simple terms, how to find peace in every situation through prayer and thanksgiving. There are times when we know we should be praying, but we just don't have words to express what we want to say to God. Trust me, it happens to all of us. When these times come upon you, remember what Paul tells us in Romans 8:26-27 about the Holy Spirit, and pray anyway. If you don't have the words to say, just stop and say "Jesus" and be still. The Holy Spirit will speak for you from your heart … and God will understand. Walking in communion with God is a *huge* source of comfort in the times when we need it most.

If you want to jump-start your prayer life and get on the fast-track to communion with God, learn to pray the Scriptures. Here's an example:

> Father, I just want to thank You that You love me (said in at least half of the Bible), that You will never leave me or forsake me (Hebrews 13:5), and that You have a good plan for my life (Jeremiah 29:11). Thank You for sending Your Holy Spirit to live inside of me to help guide me when I need it the most (John 14:16-17). Strengthen me and help me to always remember that You are right here with me, and that I don't always need to understand everything, but instead I just need to trust in You to quiet my fear and anxiety (Proverbs 3:5-6), in Jesus's name. Amen.

That is a short, simple, little three-sentence prayer, but you'd be amazed if you understood just exactly how powerful those few words can be in your life when you are struggling in some circumstance. First of all, by saying those words, you are praising God! In the first sentence, you are thanking Him verbatim for the promises you are leaning on in that moment. In the second sentence, you are thanking Him for the gift of the Holy Spirit and humbly acknowledging your need for guidance from above. In the last sentence, you are asking for perseverance and a reminder to yield your will to God's in full faith so that He can deal with the problem and you don't have to worry and stress about it. If you humble yourself, set pride aside, and get this thinking deep down into your heart, you will see stress leave your life!

I am a firm believer that God loves it when we pray the Scriptures back to Him. It makes perfect sense if you think about it. Here's why:

1. It shows you have been reading and studying His Word, *seeking* and learning the promises. That is honoring God.

2. It demonstrates that you are growing in understanding of His Word and applying the promises to your life. Understanding His Word and applying the promises to your life will lead to increased faith. Because as you *ask* Him for help, you will see results in trusting the promises.

3. And the more your faith grows, the more you will humble yourself before Him and acknowledge your need for Him. You will find yourself learning to get out of God's way, so that He can work mightily through you and in you. That is *knocking* on the door that opens to communion with God.

> But seek first the kingdom of God and his righteousness, and all these things will be added to you. (Matthew 6:33)

> Ask, and it will be given to you; seek, and you will find; knock, and it will be opened to you. For everyone who asks receives, and the one who seeks finds, and to the one who knocks it will be opened. (Matthew 7:7-8)

Remember those two scripture passages I told you about that had me so befuddled in the early days, when I was trying to find my way to get on God's intended path for me ... those two quotes from Jesus, just a few verses apart in consecutive chapters of Matthew? Now we can all understand how they work for us in our lives. *Seek first the kingdom ... ask, seek, and knock* ... and all these things will be added unto you.

> Humble yourselves, therefore, under the mighty hand of God so that at the proper time he may exalt you, casting all your anxieties on him, because he cares for you. (1 Peter 5:6-7)

> Humble yourselves before the Lord, and he will exalt you. (James 4:10)

Ditch your pride and any thoughts of self-sufficiency. Don't try to do life on your own. Humble yourself before the Lord. If you want true communion with God (and you do because it is AWESOME), you have to accept the fact that apart from Him, you can do nothing (John 15:5). If you try to do it on your own, you are going to mess it up; and you will cause yourself a ton of stress and anxiety. Learn these concepts. Trust the promises and lean on God for everything.

Here is another key to a successful prayer life that was illuminated to me through a conversation I had with a buddy a while back. I had recommended that he read the book *Defined* that I mentioned a few chapters back. We were texting back and forth on the phone, and he told me, "I know in my heart God has a plan for me. Hopefully this book will continue to show me how to know what that path is. Because it would be prayers answered. I ask God to help me, and to show me what I need to do each day because most of the time, I'm lost in what I ask for, etc."

My reply was, "I know what you mean. I have finally found the path He wants me on. It took a long time; I think mostly because I had the same problem as you are having in getting that particular prayer answered. I figured out that I was praying the prayer ... often ... and frustrated because I never got the answer. Then it dawned on me one day that after I asked ... I needed to remember to shut my mind's mouth and open my mind's ears. God doesn't talk loud ... lol. The devil is always screaming loud accusations in our ears and telling us lies about how God and the whole universe are against us ... getting our brains all disoriented and cluttered and confused. We have got to learn to tune all that noise out. That's what the Bible means in Psalm 46:10 when it says, *'Be still and know that I am God.'* Because if we aren't being still ... and, more importantly, shushing our minds and making them be still, then we can't hear God whispering to us. He doesn't compete with the devil for our attention. He tells us we are His chosen and expects our reverence in return. That's what is so awesome about this book. It creates a sense of awe in us over how treasured we are in God's eyes. Once that message sinks into our core, it controls our mind, and we can finally tune out the devil and the world. The assurance of God's unfailing love for us allows us to quiet our mind and *be still* ... and to know that His plan is a better plan!!!"

It is true that we need to regularly "be still" and quiet our minds, especially when we are reading our Bibles and talking to God. Far too often, I find myself throwing my "shopping list" at God, saying amen, and then hurrying about getting other items checked off my to-do list. I have to constantly remind myself to stop and be still before I start my daily Bible reading and as I'm praying. It is so amazing on those occasions when we hear the Spirit speaking to us. I often wonder how many times we miss those whispers because we forget to be still. Work to make a habit of being still, especially during prayer time; that is when the revelations come.

If I stop and think about it, I can still remember when I was praying for the things I have today. Pausing to think about such things always puts me in a spirit of praise. Never take God's gifts for granted. Prayer is critical in everyone's life because it reminds you Who is in control. Get into the habit of saying "Good morning, God" before you even get out of bed every morning. Talk to Him like a friend all throughout the day. Prayers don't have to be formal. Just work on keeping an open dialogue going with God all day, and before you go to bed at night, thank Him for anything you had to be grateful for during the day. I think that is what Paul meant when he said *"Pray without ceasing"* in 1 Thessalonians 5:16-18. Find a time each day to settle down and read your Bible and pray. Make time because it is *that* important; and *be still* and know that He is God (Psalm 46:10).

Heavenly Father, thank You for the gift of prayer, and thank You for the unquenchable and unending love that You have for us. Open our hearts and cause us to be in awe of the fact that through the sacrifice Jesus made for us, we are able to boldly approach Your throne at any time and talk directly to You as our loving Father. Let us understand how much You want to commune with us and open our eyes to how much we should pursue this for our own good. As we focus our efforts on seeking first Your kingdom, open our eyes so that we can stop overlooking and begin to see all the work You do in our lives every day. Help us to notice all the things that You do for us and appreciate the Source of our blessings. Thank You for promising to always hear our prayers. Help us to yield our wants to Your will as we come to understand more fully that it is You alone who knows what is best for us. Create an unstoppable desire in our lives to get and keep our lives on the perfect path You intend for us to walk. Father, we praise You for it as we ask in the mighty name of Jesus. Amen.

13

GOD'S TIMELINE

And let us not grow weary of doing good, for in due season we will reap, if we do not give up.

—Galatians 6:9

I N DUE SEASON ... GOD'S TIMELINE VERSUS OUR OWN timeline is one of the biggest sources of obstacles the enemy uses to create hills in our lives to block our communion with God. At least that seems to be the case in my life. One of the hardest concepts for humans to wrap our heads around is patience. We live in a fast-paced world and have come to expect instant gratification of our every want and need. This mind-set leads to problems in our lives almost on a daily basis, especially when we find ourselves facing some major obstacle. We want to fix it and fix it now ... and it just doesn't always work like that. Instant gratification has diminished our appreciation, gratitude, and valuing of the good things in our lives. Let's face it: when we get "things" that we didn't have to work for and want for a period of time, it is just impossible to appreciate them as much as if we did have to work and want for a time to get them. Where items we do have to work and want for a time are savored and treasured, desires that are instantly gratified are most often much less appreciated on that same scale of gratitude. It's just a fact of life.

God is *always* infinitely perfect in His timing; and we are almost always infinitely imperfect in our patience and our understanding of His good plan for our lives. He, Himself, is the greatest treasure that we can ever acquire, and He is to be savored and valued above all else. I subscribe to and daily read emails from *Desiring God*; I recommend you do the same (www.desiringgod.org). Almost every single day, there seems to be content there that helps me to deal biblically with whatever situation I might be facing in life, and I love their ministry slogan: *"God is most glorified in us, when we are most satisfied in Him."* Think about that mantra and relate it to what I said in the paragraph above. Instant gratification reduces treasuring, savoring, and valuing good things we receive in life ... and God is most glorified in us when we are most satisfied in Him. With those two thoughts as our point of perspective, doesn't it make sense that finding real communion with God *should* be an undertaking that we would need to want and seek and work to attain, so that once we attain it, we would treasure it, savor it, and value it above all ... and wouldn't that be the very definition of "being most satisfied in Him"?

Yes, God has the power to deliver instant gratification to any circumstance, but if He is most glorified in us when we are *most* satisfied in Him, it doesn't seem likely that His solution to our trials, or answers to our prayers, should be one to leave us less grateful for a gift that we will place less value on. Likewise, if a lesson, a blessing, or a demonstration of the soundness of a biblical promise coming to fruition in our life is to generate a sense of deep appreciation and lasting value in us, it stands to reason we will receive it with more gratitude if we are praying for it in faith "for a time" in the midst of a trial. This is so that it would leave a lasting impression in our soul; that is the beauty of deferred gratification. Its impact is exponentially larger in our lives, and it is much more appreciated than instant gratification.

> ...but they who wait for the Lord shall renew their strength; they shall mount up with wings like eagles; they shall run and not be weary; they shall walk and not faint. (Isaiah 40:31)

> The heart of man plans his way, but the Lord establishes his steps. (Proverbs 16:9)

> The Lord is good to those who wait for him, to the soul who seeks him. It is good that one should wait quietly for the salvation of the Lord. (Lamentations 3:25-26)

> For everything there is a season, and a time for every matter
> under heaven. (Ecclesiastes 3:1)

A few years ago, when I was in my battle with depression, and I decided to isolate myself in the middle of nowhere on the ranch where I had been guiding hunters for a few years, I had already begun seeking more of God. And I had figured out that was what was missing from my life. I was determined to find communion and the peace that Jesus promised to give me that came with it. I fell in love with the verse above from Isaiah and clung to it with all my might, much like those two quotes from Jesus in the book of Matthew, which I have talked so much about. And like those quotes, I was struggling to find the truth in it for some time. I knew it had to be true because it said so in my Bible. I just seemed to fall short daily in the soaring and not being weary departments, but I refused to give up on it.

I prayed about it and begged God to show me how it worked. As time passed, maybe a few months or so, I began to see things differently in my life. I caught myself noticing things bringing me notably more joy than they had in the past … such as sprawling sun rises or sunsets, evening thunderheads flashing their lightning bolts, seeing baby wildlife that I had been around most of my life, and even flowers on the vegetation. I found myself in awe of God's creation, similar to how I was when I was a kid. It was like every day I was noticing some random, little thing that He did "just for me." I was appreciating it, thanking Him for those little, insignificant things, and it was lifting me out of the fog of depression and self-pity I had been stuck in for so long. I wasn't sure where it was leading, but I deemed it progress of some sort, thanked God for it, and kept seeking.

> Enter by the narrow gate. For the gate is wide and the way is
> easy that leads to destruction, and those who enter by it are
> many. For the gate is narrow and the way is hard that leads to
> life, and those who find it are few. (Matthew 7:13-14)

This is another quote from Jesus that gives us a great life lesson. What strikes me most profoundly about it is that it is SO counterintuitive to the goal of how most of us live our lives here on earth. In fact, our "hurry up and get it done" culture preaches the exact opposite … get it done the fastest and easiest way possible, and then do more. That mantra is burned into our minds by the time we are in the third grade, if not sooner. Timed exams, get your homework done before you go play, etc.

If we are going to be "successful" in this life, we must strive to be "get it done" kind of people. While this mindset may reward us here on earth with material wealth, fame, power, and all the things humans spend their lives chasing after, it doesn't lead to much quality of life because attaining these things comes at a high price to our health and well-being: physically, emotionally, and spiritually. Now don't take that the wrong way. I'm not against a good work ethic, goal-setting, and striving to be all we can be in this life. There is nothing wrong with material wealth, fame, power, and all the rest, if we can achieve it with our priorities and morals in proper align-ment, and with God at the center of our lives. Granted, that's a big "IF" but it can be done, although Jesus cautioned us that *"it is easier for a camel to go through the eye of a needle, than for a rich man to enter into the kingdom of God"* (Matthew 19:24). But whether we attain all those things or not, priority and moral alignment, and God at the center of our lives, is WAY more im-portant and a much more rewarding way of living our best life than gaining all the wealth and accolades this world has to offer.

But back to Jesus's quote about the narrow gate, the hard way, and the few who find it. On the surface, this seems like an oxymoronic or contra-dictory statement, when set beside something else He stated in Matthew 11:28-30:

> Come to me, all who labor and are heavy laden, and I will give
> you rest. Take my yoke upon you, and learn from me, for I am
> gentle and lowly in heart, and you will find rest for your souls.
> For my yoke is easy, and my burden is light.

Let me start my clarification by making a point that is a noteworthy by-product of this discussion. There are no contradictions in the Bible, alt-hough if you read the whole book, it will appear there are many such state-ments that seem at odds with one another. I mentioned earlier that the Bible is not a book that can be read and then put back on a shelf like all other books. It is the living Word of God. To understand the Bible, we have to read it, study it, and allow the Holy Spirit to guide us through it to its true meaning and truth. Every word has to be read in its proper context and understood to clear up these passages that seem to contradict each other. These two Jesus quotes are a great example to help clarify what I mean in stating this.

If it's true when Jesus says, *"Come to me, all who labor and are heavy laden, and I will give you rest. Take my yoke upon you, and learn from me, for I am gentle and lowly in heart, and you will find rest for your souls. For my yoke is easy, and my burden is light,"* then how can it also be true when He states, *"Enter by the narrow gate. For the gate is wide and the way is easy that leads to destruction, and those who enter by it are many. For the gate is narrow and the way is hard that leads to life, and those who find it are few?"* Which is it, Jesus, easy and restful or narrow, hard, and difficult to find?

In answering this conundrum, let me take a moment to remind you that we are in this book to seek out true communion with God; because it will lead us down the path of God's perfect plan for our best life, where we get to live in the very same, absolute peace that allowed Jesus to sleep through the storm that was terrorizing His apostles. If we have that kind of peace in our life, His yoke is indeed easy, and the burden is indeed light. So that quoted scripture is absolutely, a hundred percent correct ... *but*, to achieve it, we have to be living in communion with God.

Now I've outlined in the previous chapters some of the difficulties and obstacles we can expect to face in getting and maintaining our communion with God. Jesus literally was born on this earth and lived a perfectly, sin-free life as a fully human being, so that He could be the perfect sacrifice for all the sins of all the rest of us humans. In the process of doing so, He faced every temptation, all the same type temptations, choices, and decisions that we deal with on a daily basis; yet unlike us, He never made a mistake. He understands that to live with His peace and in communion with God, we have to contend with the devil, our sinful human nature, pressures from society ... and I don't think I need to go any more into this list to make my point. He knows that we cannot live a perfect, sin-free life on this earth like He did. To walk in communion with God and live in the peace that Jesus left for us, we have to battle the enemy, throw out human nature (sin and pride), and walk against the grain of the godless society we live in.

Friends, the gate is narrow ... the way is hard ... and those who find it are few. Pray for strength and guidance from the Holy Spirit as you read your Bible and learn to be still and listen to His voice, so that you can be one of the few, despite the mistakes and errors we are guaranteed to make along the way.

As you seek first the kingdom, don't be discouraged, especially at first if you can't see progress happening in your life. I promise it is happening. Not one single iota of our seeking is ever wasted by God, but He just doesn't operate in the manner we are accustomed to in our world. We don't see spiritual results in the same format of time that we do in our worldly endeavors. God's timetable is completely different than ours, as are His goals for us. He is not interested in hurrying us through the training so that we can receive some sort of trophy or medal for setting a new speed record. Instead, His only interest is growing us to be more like Christ. On this earth, we will never achieve Christ's absolute perfection; it's not possible. That is why communion with God is not a prize or a trophy. Instead, it is the treasure of a journey that doesn't end until we draw our last breath on earth. God wants us to walk with Him, at His pace, through the entire journey, fully engulfed in the peace that Jesus left for us in John 14:27. That is the path for our best life, and no amount of money, fame, or fortune can make it any better than that. If we are to accomplish that feat, it is imperative that we truly learn to *believe* God and the promises of His Word, even in trials we can't understand … and that is the only timeline that God operates on.

> Wait for the Lord; be strong, and let your heart take courage; wait for the Lord! (Psalm 27:14)

> From of old no one has heard or perceived by the ear, no eye has seen a God besides you, who acts for those who wait for him. (Isaiah 64:4)

> For still the vision awaits its appointed time; it hastens to the end—it will not lie. If it seems slow, wait for it; it will surely come; it will not delay. (Habakkuk 2:3)

> And I am sure of this, that he who began a good work in you will bring it to completion at the day of Jesus Christ. (Philippians 1:6)

I mentioned previously in the section on roadblocks that there have been numerous times in my journey where it seemed everything just came to a standstill. I promise the same thing will happen on your journey. For me, these times usually seem to manifest right after I've had a new revelation of some sort, which I see as preparing me for the next leg of the journey … (my timeline). I always think, *Yay! Now I can move on to the next big thing, or God should open some new door for me now!* … (my plan). Then when a little time passes, I'll find myself frustrated that I'm still "stuck" in the same situation and circumstance that I've already conquered, and I can't seem to feel God's presence throughout the day.

Remember when I mentioned I liked banging my head into the wall? I'll catch myself asking God why are we still stuck here ... why aren't we moving on to something new? Then eventually, I'll realize I'm getting ahead of God on the path, at which time I have to back up beside Him and let Him remind me that He is in control, He sets the pace ... that He is leading me to *my* best life, and I need to quit being in such a hurry all the time, keep my focus on Him, and stop trying to get to whatever is next before He makes sure that I am ready. My obstinance never ceases to amaze me. It just seems to have no end, but I'm not giving up.

As I was doing some research for writing this chapter, I stumbled across another quote from Charles Spurgeon as he expounded on the scripture I used above from the book of Habakkuk. It was shared by Pastor Ken Silva in a devotion from 2009. I love the way the Holy Spirit worked in Spurgeon's mind, and I pray that someday I'll get there too. I've spent the whole chapter trying to spell it out in specifics, but I want to let him summarize it for me as I close this chapter:

> For the vision is yet for an appointed time, but at the end it shall speak, and not lie: though it tarry, wait for it; because it will surely come, it will not tarry. (Habakkuk 2:3 KJV)

> Mercy may seem slow, but it is sure. The Lord in unfailing wisdom has appointed a time for the outgoings of His gracious power, and God's time is the best time. We are in a hurry; the vision of the blessings excites our desire and hastens our longings; but the Lord will keep His appointments. He never is before His time; He never is behind.

> God's word is here spoken of as a living thing which will speak and will come. It is never a dead letter, as we are tempted to fear when we have long watched for its fulfillment. The living word is on the way from the living God, and though it may seem to linger, it is not in reality doing so. God's train is not behind time. It is only a matter of patience, and we shall soon see for ourselves the faithfulness of the Lord. No promise of His shall fail; "it will not lie." No promise of His will be lost in silence; "it shall speak." What comfort it

will speak to the believing ear! No promise of His shall need to be renewed like a bill which could not be paid on the day in which it fell due-"it will not tarry."

Come, my soul, canst thou not wait for thy God? Rest in Him and be still in unutterable peacefulness.[1]

We must shed pride and any thoughts of self-sufficiency and yield our will, our wants, and our timelines to God's. His plan is the best plan for our lives. All of His plan … and none of our own plan. All in His timing … and none in our own timing. We can only see it in hindsight, but His plan is *always* best, and His timing is *always* best. We have to learn to get out of His way, stay beside Him at His pace. Then, and *only* then, can we live our best life covered in the blanket of the peace that Jesus promised us.

"Come, my soul, canst thou not wait for thy God? Rest in Him and be still in unutterable peacefulness" … indeed!

Father, we don't have words to adequately express our thanks for the promises of Your Word. We stand totally in awe of the foresight You possessed to be able to include guidance for every single situation that anyone could ever face in life on this earth. We are amazed at the love You have shown and continue to show for us. We thank You that You have assured us we will find You when we seek You with all of our hearts. On our journey toward this end, open our eyes to see You for the immeasurable treasure that You are. Build both our understanding and our faith in Your promises and teach us to yield our wants and will to Yours. Teach us patience and keep our leash tight, as we struggle to fight our tendency to hurry on ahead so that we can learn to stay beside You on our journey. Show us Your pace and keep us to it so we can live in the peace that Jesus left for us. We praise You for it, in Jesus's mighty name. Amen.

---

[1] Charles Spurgeon, "In God's Time," Blue Letter Bible, October 27, 2023, www.blueletterbible.org/devotionals/faiths-checkbook/view.cfm?Date=11/03.

14

IN SUMMARY

S O, WE NOW KNOW THAT OUR ONE SINGLE GOAL IN THIS life as Christians is to walk in communion with God ... yielding our will, our wants, and our timetables to His. We want Him to lead us to our best and most fulfilling life as we simply trod along beside Him. We want to take in all the wonders of His creation, with no stress, fear, or worry, because we are clothed in the same robe of peace that Jesus wore while He was here on earth. We are committing to seek out this beautiful, blessed life simply because we now know that it is promised to us in the Word of God. We know the Word of God is true, and we are pledging to learn, understand, and trust His promises, and then apply them to every aspect of our lives; because that is how they work for us through faith. Our mission is clear, and our commitment is strong.

At this point, I sort of feel the need to make a confession. I recall as I've read "self-help" books in the past, I've tended to form an opinion of the author as I've soaked in the information shared in their manuscript. I recall entertaining thoughts such as: *Wow! This person really has things figured out. Their life must be awesome because they seem to have all the answers. I wish I could have my life all together like this person ... etc.*

That may or may not have been the case for those authors, but here's my confession in the form of a request: please don't let any such thoughts enter your mind about me as you are reading this book! Writing this book has been, without a doubt, the single most humbling experience of my life. I wrestled with God for at least a couple years trying to convince Him that He had picked the wrong guy, because my life was a self-made mess; and I had no business giving anyone advice on how to live out their God-designed purpose in life. Personally, I fail in that regard every single day.

It's a long and non-relevant story that led me to the point where I finally stopped wrestling, turned my computer on, and started typing, but I want to share something about the experience, which I can literally, just this second, see being revealed to me that is very relevant. As I was making my argument for God to find someone else to write this book, I was still focused on self. God was not the center of my life yet, but I was a couple years into my seeking, just like I've shown you how to do ... same exact baby steps in every aspect of every chapter.

When I finally sat down to start typing, I had no plan or outline. All I had was the title and the "Hills story" that is now chapter 1 in this manuscript, along with a few notes, journal entries, and text records of conversations I had over the course of a couple years leading up to that point. As I look at the file right now, it contains over 39,000 words, and it has all come together in just under four short months. The net result to me is that I have learned so much that I didn't understand when I started; and through the process of writing it down, I have identified so much more I need to work on in my own life, and seen the importance of doing so. Trust me when I tell you, I probably needed this book more than anyone else who might ever read it. I feel so blessed by the spiritual growth and knowledge I've gained that I literally don't have words to describe what I'm feeling; yet, at the same time, I feel like God just brought me out from behind the woodshed, and I'm totally in amazement and awe that He still loves me enough to keep loving me for the wretch that I am.

I'm writing this book as our country is, for the most part, shut down during the coronavirus fiasco. When I started writing, the first couple chapters came flooding out; then I went a few days without any inspiration to write at all. I came to the realization that I was focused on the turmoil in our country with all the "political unrest" and idiots rioting, burning, and looting. As an American patriot, I was angry ... to the point it was taking my focus off God. I was still reading my Bible every day, but I wasn't living with that peace in my soul that I knew I was supposed to have. I prayed about it, remembered to be still afterward, and I heard the Spirit remind me, "It's just the hills again." So, I worked out extra hard the next day to release the frustration and concentrated on getting my focus back on what God says, instead of looking at the news. Then I sat back down at my computer and quickly spit out a couple more chapters. The next day, I had lost the inspiration again. I swear, I have cycled through this at least a half dozen times during the course of writing this book.

Honestly, it blows my mind how easily the enemy can distract or side-track me ... even while I'm making a conscious effort to stay focused on my God ... even as I am trying to write a book on that very subject! It is enlightening. Every time I read the Old Testament narratives, I end up banging my head with my hands in dismay at the stupidity and lack of commitment by some of the characters in each story. They are all unique and teach us different valuable lessons but pay attention because this is how the plotline of every story goes: in one paragraph, man is blessed and praising God for His mighty deeds or works of deliverance; and in the next paragraph, that same man is running into sin or chasing after other gods. To make my point, I oversimplify and condense, of course, but read it for yourself and you will see what I mean. I used to always think, *My God, these people were idiots! How can they be so fickle? Why couldn't they just obey God?!!!*

A perfect example is the children of Israel leaving behind some four hundred years of captivity and slavery from Egypt. They had literally just witnessed all the plagues God sent on the Egyptians to force them to set His people free. They had seen God part the Red Sea so that they could cross through on dry land; then, He slammed the waters shut, drowning the entire Egyptian army who was chasing them at the time. God had provided water for them from a rock in the middle of the wilderness and fed them with bread from heaven on a daily basis. So how long did they stand fast in the promises of God after witnessing all of the above? Until Moses went up the mountain to get instruction from God. They couldn't wait for him to come back down because they were afraid, so they had Aaron build them a golden calf to worship. I'd read this story and thought, *Morons, imbeciles, idiots ... God, how could they be so stupid and forget so quickly the wonders they had seen?* And there are tons of other, similar examples.

I cited the example of Adam and Eve a few chapters back where I stated, "It's almost like people just couldn't wait to mess things up for themselves, but let's hold off on any harsh judgement for a moment because if we don't, it will come back around and bite us right on our posterior gluteus maximus." Here is why I said that: we are not one iota smarter or more disciplined in our own walk ... at least I'm not. I just proved it in telling you about my struggles in writing this "How to avoid the hills" field guide. It's completely baffling, mind-boggling; actually, how often I still find myself trying to fight my own battles or forge my own way through some obstacle instead of just *"seeking first the kingdom"* and trusting God to work it all out for me like He has promised. Yet, He never stops loving me...

Seek First ... It seems like such a simple command. I'm now quite sure that with a great amount of focus on purpose, Jesus specifically and deliberately chose those two simple, single-syllable words as the *key* to our peace and joy in Christian life, with the thought in His mind, *Surely they can't misunderstand and mess this up.* When that thought occurred to me, it was sufficiently humbling to cause me to ask for forgiveness for my ridiculing of the Old Testament characters ... and then immediately following suit in the midst of all of my "modern intelligence" ... on *so many* occasions. It's almost a daily occurrence. I know I have repeated "seek first" a lot throughout this book. *I promise I haven't stressed it enough!*

When you find yourself dealing with this realization in your own journey (and you will), don't feel bad and try to hide it from God. Instead, run to Him in repentance. I promise He will give you a big hug, dust you off, and set you back on the smooth path. Our God is sooo good, despite our continual failure to just trust Him and seek first! My most humble prayer is that you will receive at least a fraction of the blessing, correction, and guidance from reading this book that I have received from writing it.

We have a life of immeasurable peace and joy waiting for us, a life promised to be available to all who have faith in Jesus. I want to share with you one final journal entry in closing. I believe it does a decent job of recapping most of what I've tried to convey in this text:

Hindsight...Sunday morning ponderings:

Hindsight, from the backside of trial, viewed through the lens of biblical faith, never ceases to amaze me!!! Our God is so good!!! When you learn how to look at life through the lens of His eyes and lean on Him, then you can see the truth in His Word. Take "beauty for ashes" for example:

The Spirit of the Lord God is upon me, because the Lord has anointed me to bring good news to the suffering and afflicted. He has sent me to comfort the brokenhearted, to announce liberty to captives, and to open the eyes of the blind. He has sent me to tell those who mourn that the time of God's favor to them has come, and the day of his wrath to their enemies. To all who mourn in Israel he will give: beauty for ashes; joy instead of mourning; praise instead of heaviness. For God has planted them like strong and graceful oaks for his own glory. (Isaiah 61:1-3)

That scripture applies to you and to me, just as much as it did to the children of Israel in the days of Isaiah. If we are seeking communion with God, we will find beauty, joy, and praise flooding our lives. I was reading *All of Grace* by Charles Spurgeon when I stumbled across this gem. I quote:

From the right hand of God our Lord Jesus rules all things here below, and makes them work together for the salvation of His redeemed. He uses both bitters and sweets, trials and joys, that He may produce in sinners a better mind toward their God. Be thankful for the providence which has made you poor, or sick, or sad; for by all this Jesus works the life of your spirit and turns you to Himself. The Lord's mercy often rides to the door of our hearts on the black horse of affliction.

It is truth; it is where the meaning in our life comes from. As Christians, we are promised a blessed life. We are not owed, entitled to, or promised an easy life: but we are promised to be supplied with the faith, strength, grace, and mercy to be blessed, regardless of our circumstances in life. We are promised that as long as we believe God, whatever happens in our life (the good and the bad), He will work to our benefit. Jesus told us:

I have said these things to you, that in me you may have peace. In the world you will have tribulation. But take heart; I have overcome the world. (John 16:33)

Life is supposed to be hard. Our happiness, peace, and joy doesn't come from our circumstances, but from our trust in God. We don't always understand our troubles in life. They can sometimes confuse and depress us if we try to walk through them in our own strength. But hindsight has taught me (with a hundred percent accuracy) that when we look away from our circumstances and look with faith to the promises in the Bible, we can know that the back side of those trials will teach us lessons and cause us to grow. We can know that there is a reason we went through it, and the reason was for our own good. It's *always* true, every single time, as long as we hold onto His words:

> And we know that for those who love God all things work together for good, for those who are called according to his purpose. (Romans 8:28)

We can't always feel it because our human spirit is broken, and our attitudes are flawed. But once we finally understand what it means to live in communion under grace, our spirit is renewed, and our attitudes are fixed. The secret of a happy, joy-filled life of peace and blessing is to, regardless of our circumstances, learn to trust and live by these words from Jesus:

> Therefore I tell you, do not be anxious about your life, what you will eat or what you will drink, nor about your body, what you will put on. Is not life more than food, and the body more than clothing? Look at the birds of the air: they neither sow nor reap nor gather into barns, and yet your heavenly Father feeds them. Are you not of more value than they? And which of you by being anxious can add a single hour to his span of life? And why are you anxious about clothing? Consider the lilies of the field, how they grow: they neither toil nor spin, yet I tell you, even Solomon in all his glory was not arrayed like one of these. But if God so clothes the grass of the field, which today is alive and tomorrow is thrown into the oven, will he not much more clothe you, O you of little faith? Therefore do not be anxious, saying, "What shall we eat?" or "What shall we drink?" or "What shall we wear?" For the Gentiles seek after all these things, and your heavenly Father knows that you need them all. But seek first the kingdom of God and his righteousness, and all these things

will be added to you. Therefore do not be anxious about tomorrow, for tomorrow will be anxious for itself. Sufficient for the day is its own trouble. Matthew 6:25-34

It's all true, friends. Life can be harsh, so much so that we can't handle it on our own. We need help. He designed us that way so that we would learn to rely on Him for our very survival. The cool part of that is that when we learn to do so, He gives us not only mere survival but immense peace and joy ... no matter what our circumstances!

Jesus tells us "ask and it shall be given, seek and ye shall find, knock and the door will open." I believe those words a hundred percent, but here's what I've learned:

1. It's hard to find, because the gate is narrow, and the way is hard. You have to talk to your mind, not listen to your mind. Read your Bible and tell yourself God's words. Don't let your mind tell you what's wrong in your life, and whenever it tries to, yell stop it and tell yourself shut up. Tell yourself, "My God is good ... all the time! His plan for me is good, and I'm going to find it. Jesus came so that I could have life and have it more abundantly!" It says all that and a lot more in the Bible. Read it and preach it to yourself. It will teach you to calm the storms, using the power of Jesus in your own life.

2. When you receive the answer to your prayers, it may not come in the form that you had in mind. That's ok because God knows best what you need, like when a little kid wants to eat a donut for breakfast but the parent gives them an egg ... because it's better for them. Always be thankful for anything God gives you ... and He gives you everything you need. That's why I never worry about stuff. When you figure that out, you'll stop stressing about things all the time too. It's a function of trust. Believe God!

3. Asking and seeking leads you on the journey to the door you are supposed to knock on. It's the door that opens to communion with God. The door that, when opened, allows us to be completely buried in the mountain of peace that Jesus promised us.

The secret to flattening the hills in our lives is to become so totally saturated in the promises of the Word of God that our first response to anything that we encounter is to automatically look to God for direction. I have included a lot of scripture in the text of this book. I'm sure you have noticed several passages that I not only referenced many times, but in some cases quoted multiple times. I would encourage you to etch those referenced more than once into your heart as cornerstone building blocks to begin building your asking, seeking, and knocking upon. You will find many others that will speak volumes to your soul as you dig into your Bible, but those I cited multiple times are good reminders of how to use the other promises you will find. And never forget, when times come that you can't seem to feel the presence of God in your life, you need to talk to the Holy Spirit and figure out what you are doing that is causing you to feel that way, repent, and fix it. God is *always* right beside you. He will never leave you or forsake you ... *ever!*

When I read the book *Defined* that I mentioned earlier, I recommended it to many friends and acquaintances because it had a huge impact on my life through the understanding it gave me on how much God thinks of us. I was discussing it with one of my friends. Now this particular friend doesn't read in the same manner that I do. I tend to read analytically to learn information; it's just how God wired me. She, on the other hand, reads conceptually, almost like she is reading to evolve. I think her way of reading is a true gift because it's like she absorbs the information as she takes it in, as opposed to how I have to process things after I read them.

As we were discussing the book, I was amazed at the little details that she had picked up from the book in reading it just once because I had read it twice already and then felt the need to read it again to look for the things that she had seen. Then she asked me, "What stood out to you from the book?"

My answer was more general in terms, but I want to share my reply because this message is what inspired me to a new level of determination in my quest for spiritual growth. I'll explain shortly, but here was my reply:

> *God's love!* That's what stood out to me, with such clarity as I'd never grasped before ... and it awakened such a sense of guilt over the pride with which I'd lived my whole life ... up until about six years ago. My story is long and not overly relevant to the point, but it makes it more meaningful to me. But for the last six years, I've changed. I've been truly asking,

seeking, and knocking. I have truly learned what those things mean ... and I've found profound truth in ALL God's promises through that. BUT when I started reading this book and wrapping my mind around the concept that all that I've learned was His design ... just for me, it struck a new chord in my soul. I'm hard-headed by nature and have to learn things the hard way ... and when these things finally sunk in, it just moved me. Jesus loves me, yes I know ... simple, little song we all learned as kids. Too simple, too repeated, and too not grasped. We just can't understand the *love* with which He loves us. It's all encompassing, unbounded, limitless, awe-inspiring *love* that never ends ... and it never had a beginning! *Wow*! Before time began, He knew us and loved us and had a perfect plan for us and designed us to reflect His glory and the glory of that plan ... and all we do is just try to live our life the way we want, under our own strength. How can we be such idiots ... and how can He just keep on loving us and pursuing us, trying to get us to understand the depth and width and breadth of His love?!!! Most often, we don't even say thanks. That's what stood out to me..."

What is the source to finding the fuel we need to keep seeking until we persevere in finding and maintaining communion with God? *It is imperative* that we begin to understand Who He is and how He loves us. Once our minds grab hold of this and root the knowledge in our hearts, it truly changes us. His love is that powerful, and He is the only source for such love. All other sources of love pale in comparison. There isn't even a close second.

I encourage you to be tenacious in your pursuit of this real communion with God. Be hard-headed and refuse to give up seeking before you find it. There is no treasure or pleasure available in this life that even remotely compares with it ... and there is nothing else that can give you a true foretaste of what heaven is going to be like for us. Most of all, enjoy the journey. It truly is the absolute best life you can live. I'll be praying for you on your journey, and I ask that you pray for me as I continue mine. The Lord knows we need all the help we can get!

Father, thank You for loving us. Those words feel hollow to me because I've come to the realization that my human mind can't even come close to understanding what is the breadth and length and height and depth of Your love … and as a result, I know my simple words of praise fall far too short of expressing the magnitude of gratitude due to You for the love You shine upon us. Forgive my ineptness in this regard, Father, and know that it is with all the human strength I can muster that I offer this thanksgiving. God, I ask that You bless the lives of those reading this book with strength and perseverance as they endeavor to find communion with You, and the peace, blessings, and joy that comes with finding that which they seek. Open their eyes, as You have opened mine, so they are able to see the treasure that is You. I pray that we all learn to count it all as loss because of the surpassing worth of knowing Christ Jesus as our Lord. Father, I thank You for it, and I praise You for it, in Jesus's mighty name. Amen.

About the Author

Jeff D. Copeland is a simple, ordinary person who grew up from humble beginnings in the Pineywoods of East Texas. He has a degree in marketing from Texas A&M University, 30+ years of marketing experience, 20+ years-experience as an outdoor writer and 30 years-experience as a hunting guide. Among other life achievements, he has also managed ranches and whitetail deer breeding operations and sold farm and ranch real estate. Nothing about any of those facts makes him qualified to write a book detailing how an individual might come to seek out, find, and live their best life by walking hand-in-hand in a  special relationship of communion with God. It simply means that unbeknownst to Jeff, God gave him the gift of being able to string words together on a piece of paper in such a way as to paint vivid word pictures and stir deep emotions within the reader. Jeff took that gift for granted and made a decent living with it for a couple decades, thinking he was a self-sufficient, self-made man. Despite his Christian parent's best efforts to "raise him right," he had serious doubts as to whether or not there even was a "higher power" at all; much less the Loving Heavenly Father he has now come to know over the last ten years.

When Jeff's "self-made" life turned into a self-made mess causing him to hit rock bottom, he was surprised beyond measure to find out that God

IS the Rock at the bottom. It suddenly became clear that the hand of the God he hadn't really believed in had in fact been the cause of every success Jeff had ever achieved; and thankfully, also the source of every precisely-measured obstacle and trial he had ever faced in life. In that moment, Jeff came to understand that God IS love. God wants nothing more than for us to live our best and most blessed life; which He designed just for us before time began. That longing of God's causes Him to pursue us, using "life's circumstances" to nudge (or push) us towards Him until we accept His invitation. He never gives up trying to give us our best life, no matter how hard-headed and obstinate we are.

Coming to this realization created a deep sense of awe for God in Jeff and he found himself on a quest to devour the Bible to learn Who God was, who God wanted him to be, and to figure out how to be able to see the truth in all the promises of the Bible in his own life. As Jeff embarked on this journey; slowly but surely, God began to reveal how the promises work (and they all do work exactly as the Bible states); but to Jeff's dismay, there were times when nothing seemed to work as promised. Through continued diligent study and meditation on the Word, God finally gave him "eyes to see" and "ears to hear" that the truth of the failures was due to continuing battles with pride and a tendency to keep moving "self" to the center, instead of keeping God at the center of Jeff's life. That is the key to living in communion with God and living our best life under the blanket of peace that Jesus promised is available to ALL Christians in John 14:27: God has to be at the center!

As Jeff's understanding of this concept of getting and keeping God at the center came into focus, and he started fighting the daily battle to eliminate "self and pride" from the equation; he began to feel the need to write down what he was learning. He thought he was just making notes he could refer to as a reminder for times when he was struggling; but then he realized that God had a bigger plan. As hard-headed and prideful or conceited as Jeff had been for the majority of his life, he would be the perfectly imperfect example to others trying to figure out how to define that longing in their soul which nothing of this world could ever satisfy. Because if God could lead Jeff from rock bottom into the blessed life the Bible promises is available to all who believe in Jesus; there is nobody anywhere who can't be led there. Aside from being a child of God, there is nothing overly special about Jeff. He is simply a regular, everyday failing human earnestly striving to walk through life hand-in-hand with his God, who provides all, and to share the truths of the promises of God's Word with others.

Jeff and his Jack Russell, Bindi live in a small town in the Texas Hill Country.

Made in the USA
Middletown, DE
04 January 2024

46980298R00081